A VERY SHORT HISTORY OF PORTUGAL

A. H. de Oliveira Marques

LISBON
TINTA-DA-CHINA
MMXIX

© 2018, João José Alves Dias
and Edições tinta-da-china, Lda.
Rua Francisco Ferrer, 6A
1500-461 Lisbon
Tels.: 21 726 90 28/9
E-mail: info@tintadachina.pt
www.tintadachina.pt

Original title: *Brevíssima História de Portugal*

Title: *A Very Short History of Portugal*
Author: A.H. de Oliveira Marques
(updated by João José Alves Dias)
Proofreading: Rita Matos
Typesetting: Tinta-da-china
Cover design: Tinta-da-china (V. Tavares)

1.ˢᵗ edition: March 2018
4.ᵗʰ edition: October 2019

ISBN: 978-989-671-420-8
LEGAL DEPOSIT n.º 436899/18

CONTENTS

INTRODUCTION: The Origins	9
The Formation of Portugal	21
The Feudal Age	37
The Beginning of Expansion	49
The Ranaissance State	61
The Rise of the Empire	75
Apogee and Decline	89
The Tridimensional Empire	105
Absolutism and Enlightened Despotism	119
Brazil	133
Constitutional Monarchy	145
Africa	167
The First Republic	181
The «New State»	195
The Overseas Empire in the 20th Century	215
The Second Republic	227
HEADS OF STATE	233
BIBLIOGRAPHY	239
THE AUTHOR	245

INTRODUCTION: THE ORIGINS

Man arrived in the Iberian Peninsula very early on in history. Remains of cultures are plentiful in the peninsula, which helps us to trace human presence in the region back one million years. The Western part, currently Portugal, is rich in archaeological evidence from all periods.

Bronze cultures probably appeared as early as 2000 B.C., attesting to the predominance of a similar type of man, the dolichocephalies, of average height, probably of dark complexion, as well as some mesocephalies. The Iron period saw the arrival of the first Indo-European peoples. Afterwards, came the Celts and the Iberians, as well as the first highly-civilized maritime peoples, the Phoenicians (before 1000 B.C.) and the Greeks. There is little to say about their contribution to the ethnic composition of the future Portuguese. All of them were similar anthropologically, the so-called Mediterranean type of man. The same is true of other invaders who conquered the Iberian Peninsula, either in part or in its entirety: the Carthaginians, the Romans and the Muslims.

Phoenician and Greek colonization hardly touched the northern part of present-day Portugal. In southern Portugal, however, their influence was noticeable, though limited to the coast line.

When the Romans conquered the Iberian Peninsula and civilized it permanently (second century B.C. to first century A.D.), they found in the West several native peoples who they classified and labelled. Of these groups, the *Gallaeci* and the *Lusitani* were the most important, and only they prevailed in both geography and administration.

The native languages were of little or no importance in the birth and rise of Portuguese. It was the natives who learned Latin, not the Romans who learned the local languages. Two legions settled in *Callaecia* or *Gallaecia* (that is, Galicia) and remained there for some time. It is therefore presumable that the dialectal forms of Vulgar Latin spoken by the legionaries have determined or influenced the rise of Galician-Portuguese.

Yet early medieval Portuguese should not be associated with Galician-Portuguese only. The dialect (or dialects) spoken in *Lusitania* was just as important. There were nuclei of Italian colonists settled in the rising centres of the south. Thus, Roman or Italic dialects probably had a major effect on the rise of southern Portuguese.

Neither Suevi nor Visigoths affected the Hispanic idioms. The Arabs arrived early in the eighth century and with them came the second and last significant component of the Portuguese language. Some 600 words passed from Arabic into Portuguese. The Muslim conquest, however, only lasted in central and southern Portugal, i.e. in the area where Galician-Portuguese was never spoken. «Lusitanian», which we now might call Mozarabic or the language of the Mozarabs, evolved separately and under different cultural circumstances. We know nothing of its features. But it certainly had its own individuality.

By the 11th and 12th centuries, when the Mondego and then the Tagus had been definitively crossed by the Christian armies, Galician-Portuguese and Lusitanian-Mozarabic came in direct and permanent contact. It was from this encounter that the Portuguese language was born.

The Portuguese borders, as they have existed from the 13th century onwards, are not mere products of the hazards of the Christian Reconquest of territory from the Muslims. Nor were they the fortuitous result of military adventures against Christian neighbours. Their origin and permanent traits must be sought far back into the past and mostly by the Roman, ecclesiastical and Muslim administration systems.

In the first century B.C., the administrative reforms of Augustus divided the former *Hispania Ulterior* into two provinces, *Lusitania* and *Baetica,* loosely separated by the Guadiana River. From *Lusitania*, with its capital *Emerita,* the region to the north of the Douro (*Gallaecia*) was taken and annexed to the *Tarraconensis* province. For judicial purposes, each province was further divided into smaller units called *conventus*. *Lusitania* comprised three of them, named *Pacensis* (from *Pax*), *Scallabitanus* (after *Scalllabis*), and *Emeritensis* (after *Emerita)*. The first two were separated from each other by the Tagus river. An artificial border line, probably based on tribal frontiers, separated the third *conventus* from the other two. Also artificial, but nonetheless founded upon actual separation of native peoples, was the boundary between north-eastern *Lusitania* and the *Tarraconensis*. The latter province was divided into a great number of *conventus*. In the northwest there were the *Bracarensis* (after *Bracara*), the *Lucensis* (after *Lucus),* and the *Asturicensis* (after *Asturica)*.

Two aspects stand out from all these details: the division between southern and northern «Portugal» by the Douro line and an almost complete coincidence between the area of the three adjoining *conventus* (the *Bracarensis,* the *Scallabitanus,* and the *Pacensis)* and present-day Portugal.

In each province there were urban nuclei, the *municipia*, the *coloniae*, the *praefecturae*, and the *civitates*, as well as rural areas known as *gentes* or *pagi*. As time went by, distinctions between their political status and their administrative status, which derived from their origin, were gradually blurred, and the *civitates* prevailed over all the others as a general name.

Some cities emerged as centres of greater political and economic significance. It was there that Christianity, an essentially urban religion, spread more rapidly. By late Roman times, most of the cities were residences of bishops and capitals of religious districts known as *dioceses*. As a rule, in each province one of the bishops — the one living in his capital city — had a certain pre-eminence. He was called the metropolitan and corresponded to the civil head of the province. The metropolitan of *Lusitania* lived in *Emerita*, and that of *Gallaecia* in *Bracara*.

Suevi and Visigoths only brought along minor changes. The *civitas* and its adjoining land, the *territorium*, gradually replaced, for administrative and political purposes, both the *conventus* and the province. This meant a greater emphasis on the local unit and local problems, directly opposed to the existence of an efficient and real centralization. For practical purposes, the province (sometimes called «duchy», for its head was now a duke, *dux*) ceased to have any real relevance. Even the memory of it faded and left no traces in late medieval times. The weakening of provincial authority gave the *conventus* a unique status, not because it played a major role in justice or administration, but because it was reinforced by the the episcopal organization's overriding power.

The *conventus*, however, would also eventually disappear. While Christianity expanded, new bishoprics had to be founded within the same conventual area. In turn, they became the essential administrative units ruling cities and territories. If, for boundary purposes, some of the *conventus* survived, it was simply because the ecclesiastical dioceses happened to coincide with it and stopped at its borders. But within each *conventus* new fractions were now possible, following the border line of each bishopric. This was particularly true of the dioceses of *Tude* and *Auriense,* which comprised the area between the Lima and the northern frontier of the *conventus Bracarensis.* Part of *Tude* became «Portuguese» later. The diocese of Egitania, slightly to the east of the *conventus Scallabitanus* and probably a part of the *Emeritensis,* was later added to the new country.

All over the world, the Arab conquest respected and preserved the existing administrative units. Only the identifying names were changed. Emirates were established, each one corresponding to a province or group of provinces. Below the emirates there were the *kuwar* or districts, corresponding to the former *conventus* or the religious dioceses. Lesser units within each *kura* were the *quran* (sing. *qarya)* or local communities. Military reasons led to the rise of other districts or landmarks, closer to the border, encompassing several *kuwar,* and where civilian and military powers were unified under a stronger unit of command.

Thus, when the «Reconquista» started and the Christian order gradually submerged the whole of western Iberia, nothing essential had been changed in the boundaries and administrative habits, which in some cases were almost one thousand years old. No wonder that such a condition would always be kept in mind by kings, lords, bishops and communities.

The Romans, in their effort to centralize administration and to civilize and pacify the native tribes, built a wide network of roads, permanently connecting areas which until then had been more or less isolated. Easy communication became possible among all the provinces and all the *conventus.* Within this rather complex network of communications, two facts stand out and should be emphasized: first, the existence of two developed areas, one to the north of the Douro, the other to the south of the Tagus basin (thus including the northern bank of the river), separated by a vast region of sparse population and few important settlements; second, the south-north road connection which put those two areas in relatively easy contact.

The Roman road network was probably expanded after the fourth century. All the significant political and economic towns in Visigothic and Muslim times were located along the main Roman roads: capitals of provinces, all the seats of *conventus, kura* and judicial units, all the episcopal cities, and even minor urban nuclei and rural centres. During the Muslim era, this network was slightly improved, particularly in the south, where some new roads were built.

•

Before the actual formation of Portugal as a separate country in western Iberia, several political units existed within parts of her future territory. Much has been written about the impact that such realms might have had on Portugal's birth and permanence as a nation. But because of their remote past, it seems difficult to substantiate such claims.

Among the peoples who invaded Spain in the beginning of the fifth century, the Suevi played one of the most relevant roles. Arriving either by land or by sea, they reached the far northwest as early as 411, settling down in *Gallaecia* as *foederati* and gradually emerging as a strong kingdom. By 419, the Suevi alone were sharing *Gallaecia* with the native peoples, after having got rid of the Alani and the Vandals. As usual, they chose the country and turned their backs on the cities, where the Roman population was left undisturbed. Their number was obviously small, and their imprint on the land minimal. By the middle of the fifth century, they controlled *Gallaecia, Lusitania, Baetica,* and part of the *Carthaginensis,* and raided the *Tarraconensis.* Later, however, their decline became rapid. As a tributary of the Visigoths or coexisting with them in a much-reduced area, the realm of the Suevi persisted and was able to maintain a frontier line which included *Gallaecia* and the two Lusitanian bishoprics of Veseo and Conimbriga, later turned into four. The Suevi were originally a heathen people. After hesitating between Catholicism and Arianism, they chose the former, which led to a violent reaction from the Arian Visigoths. By 576, a campaign against the Suevi started. Their kingdom was incorporated into the Visigothic State (585).

For the future Portugal, only the ecclesiastical framework of the Suevi was significant. In the sixth century, two metropolitan centres overlapped with the Suevi's principal cities, *Bracara* and *Lucus,* each one with a certain number of dependent bishoprics. *Bracara* headed the dioceses of *Dumio, Portucale, Lamecum, Veseo, Conimbriga* and *Egitania.* The division line with *Lucus* was the river Lima. The interesting fact in this arrangement is that the area of the dioceses of *Lamecum, Veseo, Conimbriga* and *Egitania,* formerly included in the metropolitan province of *Emerita (Lusitania),* was now assigned to *Bracara (Gallaecia)* because of the new political unit. This assignment continued until 660, and was much later, in the «Reconquista» period, used by the bishops of Braga, with the backing of Portuguese rulers, to claim the ecclesiastical inheritance of the Suevi and thus to unite the whole territory from the Lima to the Tagus rivers.

The Muslims landed in Spain for purposes of conquest in 711. Two years later, practically all the Peninsula was under the sway of Islam. But the Christian «Reconquista» came quickly, growing from a small piece of territory in Asturias to a vast area limited at the south by the Douro basin. The victories of king Alfonso I covered all of *Gallaecia* and reached *Lusitania* south all the way down to *Veseo* (Viseu). For more than a century, most of Galicia was, if not a battlefield, at least a very unsafe frontier land, rather disorganized, with half-deserted and half-burned down cities, impoverished and sparsely populated, with all its bishops (that is, most of its real authority) fleeing to the king's court and remaining there for a long time. South Galicia, between the rivers Minho and Douro, suffered the most from these events.

It was not until the middle of the ninth century that conditions improved and were thought favourable enough for a general reorganization and new settlement. However, the Muslims returned, bringing with them new destruction and disorganization. It took the Christians seventy more years to come back to the Mondego. Dume (ancient *Dumio)* was never restored, being absorbed by Braga. Idanha was transferred to Guarda, but only in 1199 was a new bishop appointed.

Within the kingdom of Asturias (or Leon, as it was known after the tenth century), the great units for administration purposes were the so-called *terrae,* sometimes *provinciae,* and their government entrusted to a count *(comes),* also called *dux.* The old Roman and Visigothic tradition was therefore maintained and enforced. There were, of course, many other counts *(comites)* who administered smaller units, also named *terrae* or *territoria.*

From time to time, royal wills and international dissensions made Galicia «independent». From 926 to 930, Galicia was further dismembered, into two parts, the southern part being assigned to Ramiro Ordóñez, who was «King of Portugal», before inheriting the whole of his father's realm. Such short periods of separation were meaningless. They were normal events in most feudal monarchies and generally brought about no permanent pretensions of autonomy; nor were they a result of any local efforts leaning toward independence.

Late in the ninth century, the territory south of the Lima and north of the Douro, being sufficiently reorganized and too important to be kept joined with the rest of Galicia, was detached from it and entrusted to a new governor *(dux)*. Its seat was *Portucale,* and its name gradually became *Portucale* too, the word appearing for the first time in this broader sense in 938. The land of Portucale — *Portugal* in the dialect that was actually spoken — was divided further into small counties, also called *terrae* or *territoria.* The line of known *duces* started with Gonçalo Mendes. After him, a dynasty of five or six governors kept Portugal united as a true fief in the same family until the mid-11th century.

South or the Douro, the conquered territories formed another province called Coimbra, logically maintaining the old administrative tradition. It seems, however, that hereditary transmission in government was never regular here, although the same family kept it for quite a long time.

Thus, for almost two hundred years, either the whole or at least a vast part of northern Portugal was kept united under the same family, with a rudimentary central government, a «ducal» court and the predictable problems consequently arising. A principle of unity was achieved. In feudal times, this meant much more than the old Roman or Visigothic administrative units. It meant the beginning of autonomy, the first continuous assertion of political individuality opposing the kingdom of Leon.

•

In the 11th century, the central authority of the Cordoba caliphate collapsed. In its place, there appeared all over Muslim Spain small kingdoms called *taifas*. From 1012 through to 1094, six of those kingdoms rose and fell in *Gharb al-Andalus: Walba* (Huelva), *Martula* (Mértola), *Shanta Mariya* (Faro), *Baja* (Beja), *Shilb* (Silves) and *Batalyaws* (Badajoz).

Batalyaws was the largest kingdom of all, encompassing most of the ancient *Lusitania,* with the seat in *Batalyaws,* a new military town which was gradually replacing *Marida* (Merida). It lasted from 1022 through to 1094, having been one of the last kingdoms to fall. Its origin was the Lower March of al-Andalus, a successor of *Lusitania*. A continuous conflict with the *taifa* of *Ishbiliya* weakened *Batalyaws* to the benefit of the Christian advance. The entire northern part of the kingdom fell before the Christian armies of Fernando I of Leon and Castile. The Christian advance appeared so dangerous that the king of Batalyaws took the risk of begging the Almoravids for help. The Almoravids had built up an imposing empire in north Africa. Although the menace they represented to the independence of the small *taifa* kingdoms was felt, Spanish Muslims had no choice. The Almoravids landed in Spain. They did push the Christians back but decided to reunify the Peninsula under their rule. In a reversal of fortunes, the king of Batalyaws asked the Christians for help, surrendering Santarin (Santarém) and al-Ushbuna (Lisbon) (1093) to them, but to no avail. The Almoravid power was too strong to be resisted, and the whole of al-Gharb fell into their hands (1094-95). Shortly after, those two cities were recovered (al-Ushbuna, in 1094; Santarin, in 1110) and the Muslim frontier was pushed back north again to the Mondego basin.

The *taifa* kingdoms did not last long enough to impose a unification pattern on southwest Iberia. Furthermore, their ties with the rest of Muslin Spain remained unbroken, within an easy system of communication and developed economic relations. Localisms, however, increased and expanded under their existence. They might not have been powerful enough to crystallize into an independence, but they certainly helped to overthrow a yoke which was from then on deemed unsustainable. Conscious of their own small interests and oppressed by a tougher and tighter military system, the local units of al-Gharb became the northern Christians' best allies to accomplish the «Reconquista».

THE FORMATION
OF PORTUGAL

The myth of a united Spanish kingdom always hovered over the small kingdoms in the Peninsula. Well aware of this impression, some of the kings of Leon adopted the title of emperor. As «emperors», they could and should have kings as vassals. And it is this relationship between such «kings» and their «emperor» that is very revealing and helps to explain the birth of Portugal as an independent country.

By the late 11th century, several contingents of French knights arrived in the Iberian Peninsula, for the purpose of fighting the infidel and helping the Christian princes against the Almoravid threat. One of them was Henry of Burgundy who married Theresa, a bastard child of emperor Alfonso VI of Leon and Castile. He was granted the whole territory south of the Minho region as a fief, as was the way in France. Henry was bound by the usual ties of vassalage to his sovereign.

When Alfonso VI died in 1109, Urraca inherited the crown. Her second marriage to Alfonso I of Aragon brought about a civil war. Aragonese, Leonese, Castilian and Galician noblemen fought among themselves for years. Count Henry very cleverly never committed himself entirely to any of the parties, rather leaning towards whoever was on the winning side and maintaining complete freedom of action, a state very close to independence.

Until his death, in 1112 or 1114, he ceased to perform his feudal duties, but never rebelling openly. After his death, his widow Theresa inherited both the government and adopted her husband's policy. She managed to sustained relative independence.

Urraca's death put Alfonso VII on the throne (1126). He quickly reminded his aunt of her feudal tenures, forcing her into submission after a brief campaign (1127). For the first time, her son Afonso Henriques, a young man of eighteen, appeared in history. Besieged in Guimarães by his cousin's armies, he was bound to surrender and make his pledge of vassalage. He surrounded himself with a group of noblemen who opposed the rule of Theresa and her protegé, a Galician count. A rebellion in Portugal gave Afonso Henriques an easy victory in 1128, at the battle of São Mamede (near Guimarães). Theresa fled to Galicia never to return again.

From 1128 to 1137, Afonso Henriques was in almost constant rebellion against his cousin Alfonso VII. To speak of independence, however, would be anachronic. What Afonso Henriques wanted was territorial expansion. And he was clearly vying for the title of king (*rex*).

Being a *rex* did not imply independence in the sense of breaking with feudal ties completely. An emperor could and should have kings as vassals. This explains why Alfonso VII did not react too strongly against his cousin's ambition. After some skirmishes, a permanent peace settlement was arranged in 1143 which granted Afonso Henriques the title of king, but maintained all the clauses related to military help whenever necessary. Afonso Henriques' foreign policy was now at stake in Italy. He commended Portugal to the Holy See and considered himself, along with his successors, a liege vassal of the Pope's. But it took another thirty-five years for Pope Alexander III to solemnly recognize him as king and his state as a kingdom. Much had changed, meanwhile, in the Leonese monarchy. After the death of Alfonso VII in 1157, his two sons Fernando and Sancho divided the kingdom which remained separated until 1230. The title of emperor was dropped. No wonder that the king of Portugal, after 1157, felt he should have the same rights and duties as both the king of Leon and the king of Castile.

For about eighty years (mid-11th to mid-12th century) there were no enduing territorial changes in Portugal. From Minho to Mondego, most of the settlement was dispersed as required by soil and climate conditions, with a very large number of *villae* and other rural units of land exploitation. Braga was the major city in the north of Portugal, an important central point for communications. Its large cathedral was in accordance with the town's size and importance. Close to Braga in size was Coimbra, the «capital» of the south, followed by *Portucale* (Porto). All the remaining «cities» were only villages or sets of *villae* but one could hardly call them towns, even in medieval phraseology.

There is no reason to believe that the demographic revolution did not happen in Portugal as it did all over Europe in the 11th, 12th, and 13th centuries. Semi-deserted areas in Beira and Trás-os-Montes, which had never been populated before, were now occupied by small groups of settlers. The breaking down of the old Roman *villa* was accelerated, and within each *villa* the smaller units (*casais,* the Portuguese equivalent of *mansi*) assigned to one family were parcelled out for all practical purposes among the surviving heirs. It was around that time that new *villae,* in the sense of new hamlets or villages rather than the old Roman exploitation form, were founded here and there.

Most of the land belonged to the Church. The Christian Reconquest had respected property tradition and transferred the property belonging to Muslim mosques to the bishops and the newly-created monasteries. Huge grants by generous monarchs rivalled death legacies by noblemen and commoners. And the Church expanded this heritage with numerous acquisitions.

Afonso II (1211-23) was the first monarch who dared to defy the Church, enacting a prohibition against any further purchasing of land by religious institutions. The attempt failed, but Sancho II (1223-45) carried on his father's policy, not only enforcing Afonso's first laws but enacting new ones, such as forbidding private purchase by clerics and even donations and legacies to the Church. His deposition (1245) was partly a result of such measures.

The king was the second largest landowner, after the Church, and a third share was almost entirely in the hands of the nobility. It was again under Afonso II that measures challenging the power of the nobility were first envisaged. He ordered all the property titles and privileges resulting from royal grants to be presented to him to be confirmed by his chancellery.

Much smaller in area and in revenues was a fourth and last share, composed of allodial lands belonging to small freeholders and common lands exploited by agrarian or urban communities.

The social structure resulted from the typical feudal forms of landownership and land revenues. Within their estates, the lords were the highest authority for all practical purposes, even if the king maintained the rights of supreme justice. There lived a population composed mainly of serfs, bound to the land they tilled by tradition and custom, prevented from leaving it but also from being expelled from it, and forced to pay their lord a rent proportional to the annual production, to which labour services and other tributes should be added. It is true that social mobility enabled by the «Reconquista» prevented a complete stagnation of that class and helped free many serfs.

Beside the serfs, there were other farmers or labourers, as well as craftsmen and house servants, who could theoretically dispose of their persons and goods, move away from their lands, and leave their lords freely. Their ties were based on a lease contract or on the contract of hired labourers, and their economic situation was not essentially different from that of the serfs. Their only real advantage was that they were able to acquire a piece of property of their own or move within the area of the *concelhos* (the Portuguese communal precincts) where their social and economic promotion was possible. Precisely because of that, their number grew as a consequence of the «Reconquista», especially after the 12th century. The wealthiest of these people generally lived within the area of the *concelho,* which they practically governed. If they had enough revenue to own a horse and to go to war on horseback (with all the appropriate weapons), they were called *cavaleiros-vilãos* (villain-knights).

Social distinctions among noblemen seem nowadays confusing, particularly because a new nobility arose in Portugal during the 11th and 12th centuries. The leading positions in command and wealth fell into the hands of a small number of newcomers and royal favourites. Below these *ricos-homens* there was another stratum of landed aristocracy, probably descending for the most part from ancient families of free men. Much larger in number, this group or class of *infanções, cavaleiros* (knights), and *escudeiros* (squires) resented the power of the *ricos-homens* and frequently caused trouble and formed parties.

As a social group, the clergy possessed little individuality. In the upper ranks, bishops, abbots and great masters of the military orders were feudal lords, acting and reacting as members of the top nobility. Below them, a vast number of clergymen ranged downward in the social hierarchy, from lower-nobility levels to conditions of serfdom. A few were even personal serfs.

The main economic activity and source of wealth was probably stock breeding. A high percentage of the land was assigned

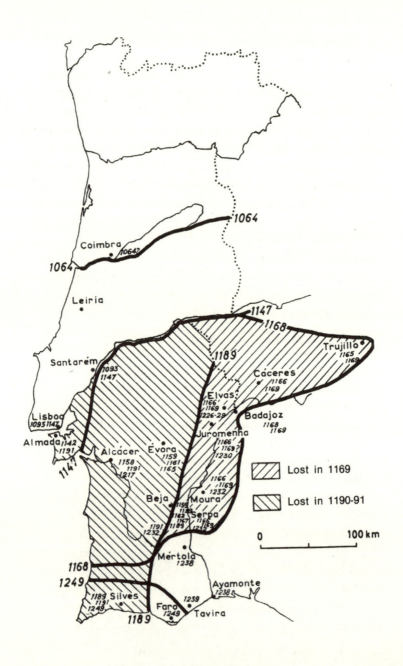

to pastures. Agrarian production was not very varied. Grain fields, vineyards and flax fields predominated. Fishing, as an economic activity, should not be underestimated. A royal policy of developing the coastline and preventing the sand from invading cultivated fields had started by the early 13th century. Several villages were thus created, or their rise fostered along the northern coast.

Most of the Portuguese economy at that time had a purely local character. Each *villa* or small group of *villae* tended to be self-sufficient and was generally successful. Economic units and boundaries were defined by the land possessions of each monastery or cathedral. A great part of the local exchange was made in kind. Money was in circulation, but it was by no means generalized or exclusive. By the late 11th century, markets were mentioned in several towns and villages, but the first fairs did not appear until late in the 12th century. The bourgeois element was weak and «burgenses» played a minor role in Portuguese history of that time. There is very little evidence of external trade. Yet, the apparently flourishing trade by the middle of the 13th century presupposes a long period of preparation and irregular activity.

For political and administrative purposes, Portugal was basically divided into *terras* or *territórios,* which corresponded to political units of feudal sovereignty. They were governed by a *tenente* of royal nomination or confirmation, who was usually the local lord and suzerain. For religious purposes, the bishoprics were naturally the great units of administration. The smallest religious unit was the parish, also called *freguesia.* The *freguesia* arose in many cases as a substitute for the old rural *palatium (paço)* when its lord was no longer a source of efficient protection or a symbol of wealth and authority for the population living in the *villa.*

Central administration belonged to the king, who was surrounded by his advisers. Under Afonso II, registers of royal acts started being used and preserved along with the seal and other insignia of power. The first general laws were also enacted by that monarch. Royal advisers, officers and members of the royal family formed a small group of people who the king frequently summoned and heard. They were his *curia* or council. When more important matters required wider debate, the king might summon a larger number of people, such as archbishops and bishops, the main abbots, the leaders or the most respected among the nobility, and the great masters of the military orders. The principle of general assembly or parliament derived from these summonses.

•

South of the Mondego valley, the Muslim civilization continued to exist and to achieve a certain cultural and economic progress.

The Almoravid victory of 1092-94 had brought about unification once again. But Yusuf ben Tashufin's glorious reign (1061-1106) was followed by weaker and weaker rulers, more repressive than before and concerned with the events in Africa. In Morocco, a new Mahdi had appeared and around him a new party of fanatics, the al-Muwahhidun (from which derived the Almohads) who began disturbing the country.

By the 1130s, the three states of Christian Spain launched an attack on al-Andalus. This movement was accompanied and actually made easier by the complete breakdown of the Almoravids. In the western part of the Peninsula, Afonso Henriques of Portugal crossed the Tagus and entered the vast plain of Ribatejo and north Alentejo. At Ourique, he finally met the Muslim defence army, which he was able to crush with some hundreds of mounted warriors (1139). It was his first great victory, but he could not take full advantage of it. It had been but a raid, unsupported by a supply system and by any reserves.

Shortly after, the second *taifa* period began. All over Spain, a wave of rebellions brought about new political units. In the western part of the Iberian Peninsula, there were units in Martula, Yabura and Baja, and Shilb, all by 1144.

Both the Christians and the Almohads profited from this political anarchy. Afonso Henriques advanced with his army and succeeded in capturing Santarin (March 1147). Approximately at the same time, the Almohads were successfully engineering the submission of al-Gharb. When, three months later, with the valuable help of a fleet of crusaders who were heading for Palestine (for the «second» crusade), Afonso Henriques decided to besiege al-Ushbuna (Lisbon), the city received no external help and fell after a three-month resistance (October 1147).

After the Tagus, the border reached the river Sado and Alentejo. But the Almohads and the king of Leon, Fernando II, decided to combine their forces against the aggressive Portuguese who were conquering both Muslim territory and areas which the Leonese thought belonged to them. United, they stopped Afonso Henriques in Badajoz, and took him prisoner.

A great invasion in 1184 again brought the Almohads to the Tagus line, besieging Santarém. Reversing his earlier alliance, Fernando II of Leon now rushed to help the Portuguese, forcing the Almohads to retreat to Alentejo, where some fortified towns had held out.

By 1189, the Portuguese attacked again, backed by a new fleet of crusaders who had called at Lisbon (for the «third» crusade). Shilb (Silves) and the surrounding areas were stormed after fierce combat. As a result, caliph al-Mansur decided to take revenge. Not only did he recapture Shilb after a long siege

(1190-91), but he proceeded north, crossed the Tagus, and raided the Estremadura region up to Torres Novas (1190). At the end of two devastating campaigns, the Almohads had placed the border line at the Tagus once more, with the sole exception of Évora, which stood alone amidst Muslim territory.

The Christian reconquest was not resumed until much later, when the Almohad power began to clearly decline. At Las Navas de Tolosa (1212), they came close to the end of their empire, when an army of Castilian, Aragonese, Navarrese and Portuguese contingents completely defeated the Almohad caliph al-Nasir (1199-1213).

In spite of this defeat, the Muslims were still strong. In Portugal, the only advantage taken during the reign of Afonso II was the conquest of Alcácer do Sal, on the river Sado. A fleet of crusaders (the «fifth» crusade) once again made this possible in 1217. But it was only in the 1220s and 1230s that the breakdown of the Almohad empire brought a new period of continuous advance. The Portuguese successively conquered Alentejo (1226-38) and part of eastern Algarve (1234-38). Sancho's brother and heir, Afonso III (1248-79), completed the conquest (1249).

The main cities in that Muslim «Portugal» were al-Ushbuna (Lisbon) and Santarin (Santarém). Next in relevance were al-Kasr Abu-Dams (Alcácer do Sal), Yalbash (Elvas), Yabura (Évora), Baja (Beja), Shirba (Serpa), Martola (Mértola), Shilb (Silves) and Shanta Mariya al-Harun (Santa Maria de Faro). Al-Ushbuna was a large town by western al-Andalus standards and an average-sized town according to general European dimensions, not much larger than its Christian rivals, Braga and Coimbra.

The south of Portugal produced cereals, fruit and olive oil. Around each town, groves and orchards, accompanied by fertile and green herb gardens, nourished the local populations and enabled some exports. The Muslims became famous for their contributions to agricultural techniques and improvements, as well as for the introduction of several new plants or implementing their use.

A relevant part in the economy was played by fish and salt. It is interesting to note that al-Ushbuna was associated with sea adventures, presumably by fishermen, and that traditional legends mentioned the discovery of inhabited lands, perhaps the Canary Islands. A shipbuilding industry may have also existed. Apparently, the Muslims of al-Gharb were considered dangerous pirates, which determined the conquest by Christians of ports such as al-Ushbuna, al-Kasr and Shilb, before the actual control of the hinterland.

The social structure of al-Gharb al-Andalus in the 12th and 13th centuries was not very different from the one in the Christian north. A class of landowners held most of the land and controlled most of the power. Unlike the northern Portuguese, however, they generally dwelt in towns or large villages, collecting their income from rent and visiting their estates from time to time, but only briefly. A few estates, or rather small holdings, were left in the hands of Christian farmers.

The State in Muslim countries was wealthy and powerful. Through the caliph and his representatives, it owned cultivated land, urban property, means of production, as well as most of the uncultivated land. This role cannot be forgotten or underestimated when trying to explain the changing conditions in royal power and fortune when the Christian kings took over everything that belonged to the Muslim State.

The second breakdown of the Caliphate in a hundred years, and the consequent rise of local units of political administration, brought about autonomous tendencies and regular hereditary governments. In many cases, heredity was maintained and even enforced in Almoravid and Almohad times as a powerful means of curbing anarchy and resisting external attacks. Local notables were entrusted with governing and succeeded in keeping it within their families for more than a generation. A small oligarchy seemed to hold power firmly and to swap positions regularly.

Jews and Christians (Mozarabs) were numerous in all of al-Gharb. Their communities were segregated from the rest of the population, lived in private ghettos and elected their own leaders.

•

Four centuries of intermittent fighting had only brought Iberian Muslims and Christians closer together. Commercial and cultural relations were matched by many political alliances and personal contacts. Bearing in mind these were medieval times and that intolerance was rife, the Spaniards presented a rather surprising example of peaceful coexistence and religiousrespect.

This attitude gradually changed. Christians were becoming the masters, and the end of Muslim rule was in sight. As a result, their former tolerance and respect, based mostly on a need to coexist, gave way to persecution and an impatience to finish the conquest. Also, the Almoravid and Almohad fanaticism did little to seal good relations and mutual tolerance.

The creation of military-religious orders in Spain, with the same purposes as those founded in Palestine, or simply the introduction of the existing ones in the Peninsula, greatly helped strengthen the ideals and goals of the crusade. In Portugal, the Knights Templar appeared around 1128. They were followed by the Hospitallers mid-century, and later by the orders of Calatrava and Santiago (both around 1170). All had a clear task to accomplish: expel the Moors, liberate the lands for Christ.

The «Reconquista» as a crusade, however, was always imperfect and very different from the Middle-Eastern wars. In Spain (and thus in Portugal too), the political aspects prevailed, and joint movements against the Muslims were rare and difficult. The crusade was felt in a local way. It was always inseparable from the royal interests in each kingdom and strictly depended upon them.

In each Iberian State, the lands south of its borders were considered the areas to conquest. Boundary details followed the existing Muslim administration pattern which, as we have seen, often went back to the Roman period. From a strictly political point of view, all the Spanish kings considered themselves lawful heirs and descendants of the old Visigothic monarchs. Consequently, every piece of land they could take from the infidel was theirs legitimately. More than a religious conflict, the «Reconquista» seemed to everyone in Christian Europe to be an affair of inheritance. The kings of Portugal appeared as legitimate heirs to rule the western part of the Peninsula.

The union of the north with the south of Portugal brought about, first of all, a population movement. The Christian victory caused a vast migration of Muslims to unconquered areas in Spain and to Africa. Nonetheless, there was never a demographic vacuum, particularly in the south. Towns and villages were not deserted. The Mozarab population, plus those Muslims who decided to stay on or were caught in the speed of the conquest, persisted and preserved life and continuity. Most of the Jews seem to have stayed on too. Many people were reduced to slavery.

We have little evidence of how quickly and thoroughly the demographic blanks were filled. It is possible that the European trend of population growth helped fill the empty houses and the half-deserted fields just by an increase in birth-rate. Migration from the north was the other obvious reason which accounted for a better equilibrium between north and south. Both kings and clergy intensely promoted the arrival of new settlers by all means available. The «Reconquista» decisively contributed to gradual social change through the mobility it implied. A new society was clearly emerging in the 12th and 13th centuries.

For himself (or his protégés), the king kept the essential core of the new conquests: cities and towns. They were all organized in self-governing communities *(concelhos)*, but their taxes and direct control, as well as vast shares of houses, kilns, presses and other means of production, belonged to the monarch.

After deducting areas such as town districts *(termos)*, the king granted almost all the remaining land to the military orders. The non-military orders and the secular Church were also contemplated.

Related to the Reconquista were also the rise and expansion of municipal organization. In the Muslim towns, where there was a considerable Mozarab population, the law recognized the organization and representativeness of Christian communities (as well as the Jewish ones) through several organs and officers. Thus, when the northerners came and conquered the southern towns, they met a traditional self-governing regulation in each of them. All over the reconquered areas there was an obvious need for new regulations. These regulations, which were granted by kings and lords (Church and nobility), were called *forais*. They rarely created new institutions and were little concerned with municipal organization. Their main goal was to define and specify taxation and organization of justice.

The *forais* should not be confused with communal charters. They did not create communes, the principle of which was very far from the Iberian tradition of community government. It is true that self-rule was accepted, but only to a limited extent.

Self-administration was greatly reduced by a rigid system of taxation and a limited sphere of local justice. The king had the right to interfere frequently.

THE FEUDAL AGE

Afonso III and his two immediate successors, Dinis and Afonso IV, were able monarchs and ruled for long periods. They were followed by Pedro I (1357-1367) who ruled peacefully from 1357 to 1367. While heir to the Portuguese throne, he fell in love with Inês de Castro, tragically killed on royal orders. He was a typical figure of the late Middle Ages, very much concerned with the administration of justice, in close contact with his people, and loved by them in spite of his acts of cruelty and madness. He also began the process of «nationalizing» the religious orders when he made his illegitimate son João (the future John I) the Grand Master of the Order of Aviz (1363).

This peaceful interlude came to an end with Pedro's son Fernando I (1367-83). Taking advantage of the troubled situation in Castilian political affairs, Fernando claimed the throne for himself. With help from the British, he fought three successive wars with dubious results as a whole.

Both the wars and the international religious schism of the 14th and 15th centuries had a tremendous impact on Portugal. Social problems, which Afonso IV and Pedro I had succeeded in containing, now gave rise to a general state of discontent, particularly among the merchants and the lower classes. Only the nobility gained some advantage from the wars and presumably supported Fernando's ambitions or even fostered them.

Leaving no male heir, Fernando's throne was duly inherited by his only daughter, Beatriz, whom he had married to John I, King of Castile. Marriage clauses clearly entrusted the regency and the government of the realm to the unpopular queen-mother Leonor Teles until a son or a daughter was born to Beatriz. Whatever the circumstances, the two kingdoms were to live permanently separated.

Political manoeuvring and ambition forced the king of Castile to invade Portugal and to take over power. Backed by the lower ranks of the bourgeoisie, João, Master of Aviz, King Pedro's illegitimate son, proclaimed himself regent and defender of the realm *(regedor e defensor do Reino)* and asked England for help. John I of Castile invaded Portugal, reached Lisbon, and besieged it, in vain, for four months (1384). In a second stage of the war, he was badly defeated at Aljubarrota (1385). Unimportant skirmishes continued to occur over the following years, then a truce was signed and was successively renewed. Meanwhile, the Master of Aviz had proclaimed himself as king at court as John I (1385).

Both the rebellion and the war with Castile were decisive events in Portuguese history. They were the great test to its independence and brought noticeable changes in the social structure of the country.

Victory for the Master of Aviz resulted in a new dynasty and a new ruling class. John I (1385-1433) surrounded himself with skilled legists and bureaucrats and looked for support among traders and artisans. However, he could not prevent the rise of a new and strong landed nobility, partly a result of the concentration of estates and privileges among very few. The leader of this new class of feudal lords was Nuno Álvares

Pereira, a former war hero who he had appointed as his constable. When Nuno Álvares Pereira retired to a monastery, his son-in-law, Afonso, an illegitimate son of the king himself, took over as the head of the new aristocracy. To counterbalance his power, John I (and, later, his son Duarte) generously endowed his legitimate family: two of John's sons were made dukes and three others were given leadership of the wealthy religious-military orders.

After 1411, John I included Duarte, his firstborn and heir to the throne, in the government of the country. Together, they organized a plan of military expansion in North Africa as a way of channeling the turbulent energies of the aristocracy and securing good profits for them and the bourgeoisie. Under the command of the king, the constable, and most of the nobility, the Portuguese attacked Ceuta, in Morocco, and easily captured it (1415). They soon realized that Ceuta was useless on its own, and that they should either abandon it or conquer more towns and hinterland in North Africa.

The new monarch, Duarte (1433-38), hesitated for a while but finally yielded to the war party. A second expedition was prepared to attack Tangiers but utterly failed (1437). Almost surrounded by the Moors, the Portuguese were allowed only to embark, leaving hostages, one of them Prince Fernando, Master of Aviz, who died in captivity. The king died soon after and his eldest son, Afonso V, a child of six, ascended the throne.

After a brief civil war, Prince Pedro, brother of the deceased monarch, took over the regency. He was forced to strengthen the power of the main aristocrats. He ruled for seven years (1441-48), a troubled period of political unrest and interference in the internal politics of Castile. Finally, Afonso V, becoming of age, dispensed with his services and promptly accepted his uncle Afonso's advice and influence. Pedro, forced to rebellion, rose up in arms against his king. He was defeated and killed at Alfarrobeira (near Lisbon), along with most of his followers (1449).

•

Vassalage, as an institution, was well-established in Portugal by the 13th, 14th and 15th centuries. The small size of the country and the fact that the monarch was one of the largest land-owners explain the relatively large number of direct vassals, who accounted for the monarch's growing strength. Royal grants in the form of a benefice were called *préstamos*. Originally, they were not hereditary, but as time went on, the right of inheritance became the general and accepted practice. Many royal grants began to take the form of *morgadios* or *morgados* (entailed estates), which implied inalienability, indivisibility and perpetual succession within the same family. The word *honra* seems to have been applied to a seigniory of any description, even an allodial one. Royal grants to the Church were often called *coutos*, a word meaning the complex range of privileges and immunities which the estate would enjoy. Among the fiefs held by lay vassals and by the king himself, there were parish churches, abbeys and chapels, the so-called *padroados*. Their lords, who often had been the founders of those pious institutions, held the profits of the title and the endowments of the Church and, in some cases, even the income which came from offerings of the faithful, such as church dues.

The country's modest size and the peculiar circumstances of Portugal's birth and growth always prevented a thoroughly-developed feudal organization. The king had the last word in all the seigniories in the case of high justice. By the 13th century, he launched a sort of program destined to curb immunities and the full autonomy of the feudal lords. The confirmation policy of Afonso II was accompanied and followed by successive inquiries (*inquirições*) which lasted until the late-14th century, but which reached their peak under King Dinis.

By the 14th century, other royal acts tended to curb the expansion of the seigniorial regime. The king warned the nobility against jurisdiction abuses, sent his officers to stop the creation of new *honras,* and forced all the nobles to prove their feudal rights. The right of feudal justice was denied to all the *honras* created after 1325, with the exception of some dozen lordships. Also, royal grants were often restricted to legitimate descendants, and even then to male descendants only (*lei-mental*). Some noble families, however, managed to be exempt from it, particularly the powerful house of the Count of Barcelos, King John's illegitimate son, future Duke of Bragança. Monarchs threatened their own interests with some very generous grants. Royal princes, for instance, were given important appanages, which sometimes made them rivals of the king. By the late-14th century, the Meneses family, as well as three or four others (including the same Meneses and the Braganças) during the 15th century, could be compared in wealth, prestige and military power to some of the typical feudal lords of France or Germany. It is true, however, that their power did not endure and was rather an anomaly in a small country like Portugal.

By the 1200s, Portugal's population probably did not exceed one million inhabitants. An important development of the 13th and following centuries was the coastal settlement. Small fishing villages appeared here and there, some spontaneously, some as a result of royal or seigniorial acts. They helped create a maritime tradition and fishing skills which would prove decisive to the future of Portugal. In the north, only the town of Porto deserves our attention. Commerce and artisanship worked together in the rise of this city; with its relatively important group of authentic burghers, Porto's development was very close to that of typical European communes. Although small in area and in population, Porto was a wealthy town, and its affluence was based on «modern» forms of economic expansion.

However, the growth of Lisbon was the truly outstanding demographic feature in late-medieval Portugal. As important as Coimbra, Braga, Évora or Silves in the 12th century, Lisbon moved clearly ahead a hundred years later, with four or five times more inhabitants and building space than any other city by the late 14th century. Lisbon became the centre of Portugal's economic, social, political and cultural life. It often became synonymous with Portugal herself. Along with this fact, there was another important constant in Portuguese history, namely the contradiction between the size and means of the capital city and those of the other smaller centres.

The development of Lisbon, and other minor towns, obviously accompanied the development of trade, both external and internal. In the 1200s, the western coast of the Iberian Peninsula was connected with most west European markets. The Portuguese arrived in the British Isles by the late-12th century. Their main destination was London, where they seem to have had intimate contact with the king and his court. Their most important operational base, however, was Flanders. By the late-13th century, the Portuguese were firmly established all over western Europe and seemed to control most of the trade with Portugal.

Portuguese exports consisted of fruit, salt, wine, olive oil and honey, and some raw materials. From England, Flanders and France, Portugal received mostly textiles. Another area of Portuguese international trade was Spain and the Mediterranean world. From the 1270s onwards, Italian merchants settled in

Lisbon and in other Portuguese ports, binding Portugal to their complex network of international contacts and settlements. It was them who improved the Portuguese fleet, and their impact on naval techniques may have had some significance on Portugal's expansion in the 15th century.

The growing complexity in life and politics made it necessary to create new offices in government and administration. Still more important were the changes introduced in the system of relationships between central and local administrations. Each monarch's supreme goal was to achieve centralization; the main goal of each municipality, on the other hand, was to defend the rights of self-rule (as limited as they might be). This conflict, which was particularly fierce during medieval times, always ended in favour of the king.

In the history of the medieval parliaments, one of the top places undoubtedly belonged to the representative assemblies of the Iberian Peninsula. By the late-12th century, the *cortes* in Castile already included people's representatives. In Portugal, however, there is no clear evidence of such participation before 1254. The summoning of popular representatives (that is, delegates of the notables, mostly landowners and from some *concelhos* only), although it attested to the growing importance of the «third order» in the life of the country, should be understood mainly as a royal expedient to secure extra taxation. This, as a rule, was the major reason for assembling the people, at least during the 1200s and early 1300s.

There is some evidence of the existence of schools in the Portuguese cathedrals, at least after the 11th century. Although their only purpose was to prepare future clergymen, their role in the general framework of public education should not be forgotten. Besides these episcopal schools, there were classrooms in many monasteries. In 1288, a group of clergymen asked Pope

Nicholas IV to confirm the creation of a university, which the king had agreed should be established in Lisbon. The university was intended to be, above all, a sort of superior education school for future clergymen.

However, much more important than the «official» culture taught at schools and the university, was the one that noblemen, clerics, and even commoners obtained elsewhere. Learned tutors were present in every manorial house, often brought from abroad. It is well-known that the royal courts, at least after Sancho I (1185-1211), welcomed minstrels who toured the country, or who came from abroad, and they were an important focus of culture, especially for poetry and music. Their great epoch was the century between 1250 and 1350, but evidence of much earlier compositions suggests a long period of incubation going back to the 12th century or even before. Galician, Leonese and Castilian authors competed with the native Portuguese.

All this cultural development decisively improved Portuguese as a language, making it fit for a national role. By mid-13th century, Portuguese was already being used as the language of many public and private documents. Later in that same century, it was officially adopted as the official written language, replacing Latin, and it quickly took its place even in many ecclesiastical deeds.

A large part, if not most, of the immense booty accumulated by kings and lords during the «Reconquista» was invested in religious buildings. This fact explains the tremendous number of cathedrals, abbeys, parish churches and small chapels built in a relatively poor country, as Portugal was. It also explains why the major period of building activity coincided with the hundred years from the mid-12th to the mid-13th century. If the dioceses, the Benedictines and their followers (Cluniacs and Cistercians), and the military orders were generally associated with the Romanesque or with a hybrid Romanesque-Gothic style, the new religious orders (Franciscans, Dominicans and others), founded in and after the 13th century, built their churches and monasteries within the framework of the new Gothic style.

•

There is no evidence of a general crisis in Portugal before mid-14th century. In 1340, prices of industrial products remained high, and comparisons were made with happier periods when prices were lower. Nonetheless, the king and his advisers seemed worried by social issues. The aristocracy was spending too much and heading toward ruin. On the other hand, a bourgeoisie flourished, vying with the nobility for all the signs of hierarchy and affluence. Real estate no longer provided a sufficient source of top revenues and could not compete with profits from trade and artisanship. It was clear that the nobility was struggling with adjustment. Unable to face the new realities, to invest in trade and in other profitable activities, the nobles seemed to be attached to and longing for a period of easy prosperity, resulting from the «Reconquista». The same law of 1340 also revealed a certain restlessness within the ranks of the lower classes, expressed by the breakdown of feudal stability and the rise of a mobile labour class.

Accounts of the Black Death of 1348 give a much clearer picture of what was going on. From late September to the beginning of 1349, the country was ravaged by the plague, which killed an undetermined number of persons, perhaps one-third or more of the whole population. Its consequences were, first of all, demographic. The pestilence decimated towns and monasteries primarily and all over the country. After this first impact, the demographic effects of the plague were felt in migratory movements. People from the countryside moved to the cities, and people from smaller towns decided to look for a better life in Lisbon, Porto or Évora. New plagues, which occurred throughout the 14th and 15th centuries, killed more people and weakened several generations. The late-14th and the first half of the 15th century brought about no increase, and even witnessed a decrease, in the number of inhabitants.

The social aspects of the crisis seem clear. The towns were affected by an increasing number of migrants looking for work and for better life conditions. The economic and social readjustment brought unemployment or unfavourable conditions for most of those who were constantly coming into the city. What happened in Lisbon was typical: social grievances brought on the riots of 1371, the revolution of 1383-85, and the rebellions of 1438-41 and 1449, to mention only some of the best-known events. Porto also rebelled in the mid-14th century. Social unrest provided enough soldiers and adventurers for the various wars against Castile in 1369-97, the 15th-century expansion in North Africa, and the great voyages of discovery.

In the countryside, there was also a shortage of workforce. All over Portugal, numerous agricultural units, villages and small towns were half-deserted or thoroughly unproductive. Noble landowners, monasteries and rich farmers looked in vain for labourers. If a great number were dead, many others simply refused to work under the existing circumstances. A series of acts between 1349 and 1401 forced rural and non-rural labourers to work for the same salaries and in the same way and place as they always had. A system of passports was created to prevent open housing, and workers were apportioned among the proprietors. In spite of this and other local regulations enacted in the late-14th and early-15th centuries, the trend toward labour freedom, or at least greater labour freedom, continued. One hundred years later, a significant, if not decisive, part of all labour was entirely free, and employment was based on revocable and temporary hiring contracts.

Another aspect of the 14th-century crisis was noted in agricultural production and the landscape. Unproductive lands became excellent game preserves and pastures. Shortage of grain gradually became a subject of general concern. The number of wheat crises grew in the 1400s. The towns, particularly Lisbon, as well as some country regions, periodically suffered famines or extreme shortages of bread. To meet the lack of grain and the grain demands in the growing cities, a regulated policy of ever-increasing imports from abroad came into existence.

The decline in the crop output was probably accompanied and even provoked by an increase in some other agricultural products, such as wine and olive oil. By this time, wine exports from Portugal started playing an important role in the country's economy.

The Black Death and the many other plagues which ravaged Portugal, as well as all of Europe, after the mid-14th century, stressing the anguish of imminent death as never before, brought about tremendous social and economic changes. Free landholders, both of plebeian and noble descent, left their possessions to the clergy in an attempt to buy salvation. However, the clergy was not properly equipped to deal effectively with this sudden concentration of property. Many lands were left unexploited, disorganized, unproductive or less productive than before. Taxation by the crown or the municipalities naturally ceased, the Church being privileged and its lands tax-free. Royal or municipal revenues consequently suffered.

The impact of the crisis on currency was perhaps greater than on any other areas. After the 1350s, devaluation of money only stopped in 1435. In 1435-36, King Duarte succeeded in stabilizing the currency, although the trend toward devaluation persisted. To avoid complete economic paralysis, many payments were often made in foreign currencies or simply in kind. It seems that the great beneficiary was the middle class of the urban nuclei. They saw their profits greatly increased and invested them in fruitful undertakings and land. They also took over power or consolidated it in some important *concelhos*, such as Lisbon, but they were never able to control the local administration in most of the country. This was firmly in the hands of the old knights-villain.

One of the political results of the crisis was to tighten the ties between king and country. The new epoch required constant consultation with the people, as it required larger contributions of funds by the people to their monarch. Social instability brought about disorder, restlessness and a general claim for justice. Summoning the *cortes* became a matter of course for all the rulers over a period of more than one hundred years. John I was «elected» at *cortes* and became dependent on them for quite a long period.

THE BEGINNING OF EXPANSION

Several inventions in the art of navigation were decisive for the great discoveries. Some were already known by the early-14th century: the central rudder fixed to the sternpost of the keel, the compass, the portolan chart, the triangular or lateen sail, how to sail close-hauled or obliquely, etc. By the first half of the 15th century, a new type of ship, the caravel, had come into existence. The Portuguese had gradually improved it and it was ideal for long-distance voyages, far from the coastline. This caravel of the 1400s continued to evolve until the 16th century.

A vast corpus of astronomical and mathematical science had slowly emerged from long centuries of Muslim, Jewish and Christian study, essentially based on the achievements of the Roman world. The Muslims had created an extensive and complex terminology which covered all fields of science. They had kept alive the Greek doctrine which stated that the earth was spherical. They calculated the length of the meridian's degree with remarkable accuracy. They improved the ancient astrolabe.

Geographical knowledge was shared, to some extent, by scientists, seamen and traders, but in different ways. The west African coast was known beyond Cape Bojador (26,5° N). Both the Canary and the Madeira islands had been visited by westerners. North African inland was described as far as the south Sahara with plenty of detail on its oases, caravan routes and native kingdoms. To the west and northwest, geography was less precise. Christian scholars reported the existence of islands inhabited by fabulous monsters. Now and then, a piece of land appeared in the 14th- and early 15th-century navigation maps that roughly coincided with Iceland and vaguely echoed the Norse discoveries and settlements.

More than any others, however, the Arabs and some of their historically-recorded voyages in the Atlantic accounted for the presumed existence of land to the west. Before the 12th century, some «adventurers» (as they are mentioned in Arab historiography) departed from Lisbon, discovered a number of inhabited islands (probably the Canary Islands), and went back home. Other Arab or black travellers from Muslim areas seem to have reached the island of Sal in the Cape Verde archipelago. It is possible that Madeira and the Azores were also discovered (or rediscovered), but both archipelagos lay too far from the coast and held little economic interest as a permanent settlement.

All such islands and lands, both real and imaginary, had a tremendous impact on the Portuguese voyages of the 14th and 15th centuries. They provided a strong stimulus and a definite goal for many voyages of discovery, while filling people's minds with precise (or so it was believed) and rich descriptions of new lands.

The other side of the coin revealed appalling stories related to such lands and surrounding seas. Transmitted or coined by the Arabs, the legend of the Sea of Darkness described an ocean populated with numerous monsters and engulfed in permanent darkness, where all the ships would be wrecked by huge waves or boiling waters. For a long time, the medieval Portuguese, like the medieval Europeans in general, hesitated between the desire to go further west and south, and the fear of never returning.

Asia and its mysteries provided another source of appeal. From Asia came the much-desired spices, as well as dyestuffs, ivory, precious stones and all kinds of sophisticated commodities. Medieval geography had Asia starting at the Nile, not at the Red Sea, thus including most of modern Ethiopia. It also greatly broadened the sense of the word «India», a part of which encompassed present-day northeast Africa. There were several «Indias» and in one of them a great Christian emperor ruled over a vast territory, densely populated. Immensely rich and powerful, he was known as Prester John, for he was at the same time a priest and a king. This myth of Prester John was to prove of enormous importance in understanding the goals of Portuguese expansion and the ways in which it was directed. By the 15th century, Prester John had been recognised as the sovereign of Ethiopia, after some direct contact was attempted and achieved by both sides. The means of reaching Ethiopia from the west or the southwest, however, remained the object of much controversy, and very little continued to be known of Prester John's real power and wealth.

Most of this geographical knowledge was passed on to the Portuguese not only by the commercial and political currents connecting them with the rest of Europe, but also by the Portuguese ambassadors, travellers and pilgrims who returned home. Of particular importance were Prince Pedro's voyages in several countries and courts of western and Central Europe (1425-28), and perhaps Prince Afonso's pilgrimage to the Holy Land around 1410, as well as the embassies sent to the ecumenical councils of the 1400s.

For a long time, the Portuguese voyages were neither extensive nor systematic, and were not carried out with continuity.

For much more than a century, fishermen from the south of Portugal, through several generations, went farther and farther in their search for fish, whales and booty. Slowly but gradually, they perfected their sailing methods and their ships, and their skills were passed on from father to son. When, at the dawn of the 15th century, other circumstances permitted a greater consciousness of what had been achieved, and when enterprising merchants, noble lords, and the king himself required trained crews for their new undertakings, they found them ready and in sufficient number to be diverted from pure fishing tasks to more complex enterprises.

Technological advance and skilled manpower were, nevertheless, insufficient to back a continuous effort at systematic discovery and exploration of the unknown world. Much deeper and stronger influences had to intervene, as well as a favourable combination of conditions; in short, a favourable conjuncture had to exist. This happened during the first half of the 15th century. Europe was short of gold. All over the continent, the gold output had steadily decreased from the mid-1300s onwards, while purchases in the East had gone up almost as steadily. Coin debasements had reached unprecedented levels in Portugal, as we have seen before, and this «hunger» for gold (as well as for silver) was felt particularly in the first quarter of the 15th century. Now, the West knew very well that there was gold somewhere in Africa, south of the Sahara, because the Arab and Arab-controlled caravans brought it to the Muslim world. In order to procure it, there seemed to be two possible ways: either to secure control of some north African entrepots — which partly explains the Portuguese attacks on Morocco — or to attempt direct contact with the peoples south of Islam — which partly accounts for the Portuguese voyages of discovery.

Other motivations, though debatable, may have played a minor role: for instance, the grain shortage, which directed attention to the bountiful Moroccan harvests; or the rising sugar plantations in Portugal, producing their first profits and suggesting the conquest of some rich sugar fields in Morocco; or the search for slants, «fashionable» again in the late Middle Ages, rediscovered as a profitable undertaking both for home labour and for export; or the need for dyestuffs and shellac for the textile industry; or the prospect of finding skins and leather, believed to be abundant in North Africa.

In the 1100s, the ideal of the crusade had captivated the Iberian Peninsula and gradually entered the minds of kings and warriors. The common fight against the Almohads in the early-13th century, the enterprise which carried Afonso IV and a Portuguese army to Salado in 1340, looked very much like a crusade, though with an Iberian colour and flavour. In the early 1400s, the Portuguese had thought of conquering Granada; instead, they launched their attacks on Ceuta and Tangiers. The conquest of any Muslim lands was a crusade *per se*. In conquering Morocco, they were simply pushing back the infidel and recovering lands which had once been Christian. Political expansion and imperialism was considered a legitimate means to convert the unbeliever. So it was no wonder that the Church approved of Portuguese expansion and gave it the warmest blessing. Successive papal bulls backed the Portuguese military projects or conquests, labelled them holy «crusades», invited all the Christian rulers to help, and granted indulgences and even a share of the Church revenues — an ever-coveted resource.

Local Portuguese interests also played a part. Fishermen and traders from the Algarve did not necessarily agree with the goals and methods of Lisboners or other northern Portuguese. The municipalities, with their own selfish and narrow-minded objectives, often contributed to odd and apparently unexplained occurrences, slowdowns or hasty undertakings. The same happened with feudal lords (both as a class and individually), with the religious orders and with the king. No «national» enterprise took place before the late 15th century, when most of the expansion was, in a way, «nationalized» and «monopolized» by the crown. In its earlier phase, the Portuguese expansion should be regarded rather as a series of individual or small-group initiatives.

This whole question brings about the much-debated problem of leadership. What part did a man like Prince Henry (Henry, the Navigator) actually play?

During most of his lifetime, his main concern and ambition seem to have centred on Morocco and on a systematic plan of military conquests in that territory. Apart from Morocco, he never travelled anywhere, in contrast to some members of his family, who were familiar with Europe and its problems. Nevertheless, like many aristocrats of his time, he seemed interested in astrology and astronomy, mathematics and nautical science. He surrounded himself with a few scholars, in addition to Jewish doctors and Italian experts on trade. As a typical prince of the late Middle Ages and early Renaissance, he welcomed foreigners, listened to them and displayed his generosity in gifts and awards. More than a scholar and a scientist himself (although he was learned and talented), he seems to have been a model lord, always surrounded by faithful clients and praised by them. Later in his life, the interesting and unexpected results of the discoveries probably developed and stimulated his desire for greater knowledge and more precise achievements. The voyages of discovery, though they may have interested Prince Henry, were nonetheless primarily regarded as a way of increasing his estate and rents.

Gradually, Henry became deeply connected with seafaring and to sea people. Many of his knights and squires owned ships or controlled maritime activities. They were all entirely dependent on him as their feudal lord and commander-in-chief. He was in a unique position for launching a vast plan of maritime expansion, once he decided to do so.

Yet there is no evidence of such a plan for many years. It seems fairly well-established that of all the known voyages ordered between 1415 and 1460 (when Henry died), only about one-third were due to his initiatives. The other two-thirds were directed by the king (John I, Duarte, Afonso V), Pedro, the prince regent, feudal lords, private merchants and landowners. The same was true of the economic exploration of newly-discovered lands. Without obliterating Prince Henry's part, this fact reduces his leadership to a more human and medieval dimension.

•

Records of 14th- and early-15th-century voyages of discovery are rare and scattered. In the late-1200s, a Genoese expedition departed from Italy heading for the West African coast, crossed the latitude of the Canary Islands and disappeared without a trace. Early in the 14th century, a second Genoese voyage reached the same islands. By the middle of the century, Italian merchants in Lisbon succeeded in convincing King Afonso IV to subsidize a three-ship expedition to the Canaries. The expedition visited all 13 Canary Islands, and probably the archipelago of Madeira as well. For the first time in cartography, a famous Catalan portolan chart of 1339 correctly reported most of the isles which actually exist in both groups, with many referred to by their modern names. The Canaries were inhabited by native tribes. The archipelago was rich in economic possibilities, which explains the Portuguese and Castilian efforts to rule the islands. The long contest for final control lasted for more than a hundred years.

Things worked out differently with Madeira. It seems that the Portuguese did not pay too much attention to those uninhabited islands until the early-15th century. In 1417, however, the Castilians sent an important expedition to the isle of Porto Santo. This time, the Portuguese responded quickly and decisively: in 1419 and 1420, two expeditions left from the Algarve and occupied Madeira and Porto Santo for good. It was the real beginning of the great Portuguese expansion overseas.

By the 1420s, the Portuguese were thoroughly familiar with the west Moroccan coast. They were also familiar with the Atlantic around both the Canary and Madeira archipelagos. Whenever they sailed a little farther west, they knew they had trouble in getting favourable winds to take them back home, unless they headed northwest and then caught the trade winds blowing from the west. In one of these detours, around 1427, a pilot named Diogo de Silves (another Algarvian) perceived the island of Santa Maria, then that of São Miguel, and possibly five more of the Azorean islands.

The discovery of the west African coast was the main goal of the early-15th-century voyages. Somewhere south there were the famous «gold river» and the gold mines which supplied all of Islam. Several ships were sent by the Portuguese in the 1420s and early 1430s. In 1434, Gil Eanes sailed around the famous Cape Bojador, went on for a number of miles, and returned with the news that, for the purposes of navigation, the world did not end there.

After that, the discovery of the West African coast proceeded more rapidly. In the following year, Gil Eanes, along with Afonso Gonçalves Baldaia, crossed the tropic of Cancer (23.5° N) and reached what they supposed to be, and therefore named, Rio do Ouro (Gold River, now Rio de Oro in Saharawi). There they got the first samples of what they were primarily looking for: gold. In 1441, Cape Blanc, in present-day Mauritania, was reached by Nuno Tristão. This same navigator was probably the first to reach the mouth of the Senegal, then on to the Gambia and Salum Rivers. Other navigators discovered Cape Verde (Green Cape).

The pace of discovery did not slow down in the 1450s. Along the coastline, pilot Diogo Gomes and several others reached Guinea and Sierra Leone. Early in the following decade, or perhaps even earlier, Pedro de Sintra went as far as the latitude of what is now Monrovia (6.5° N), where the coastline curved unmistakably eastward. Off the coast, the Cape Verde archipelago was also explored in the 1450s and early 1460s.

In the North Atlantic, too, Portuguese seamen were attempting new discoveries, in search of the legendary lands indicated on the maps or told of by oral tradition. In one of those travels, they discovered the two westernmost islands of the Azores, invisible from the rest of the group. And they certainly arrived at the Sargasso Sea and gathered enough data and experience to draw a very complete and precise map of the Atlantic winds and currents, which would be used by all future navigators.

•

In the 1420s, the fear of a Castilian takeover led the Portuguese to decide on Madeira's permanent occupation. The social and economic structure of the mainland was introduced in the new islands without any major changes. Either on his own initiative or simply following instructions, João Gonçalves Zarco divided the archipelago into three parts: one for himself and the other two for each of his companions, Tristão Vaz Teixeira and Bartolomeu Perestrelo. In each of the shares, the «lord» was entitled to grant lands, either in a quit-rent lease system or as full property. Effective occupation and cultivation by a certain deadline were required.

Initially, the islands were dependent on the crown. In 1433, King Duarte I donated them as a sort of fief to his brother Henry. Spiritually, the isles were given to the Order of Christ, a sophisticated way of granting all their ecclesiastical revenues to Henry too. As lord of Madeira, Henry created a system of three perpetual and hereditary captaincies, which he entrusted to the three existing local «lords» accepting their original allotment. The *captains*, or *captain-donataries,* were to exert jurisdiction on Henry's behalf; they could grant lands to settlers, and they were given the monopoly of the means of production and sale of salt, as well as the tenth on the tithe belonging to the lord.

Dragon's blood, wood and other dyestuffs were among the settler's first exports. Fish provided the basis for local nourishment. Then, a persistent and well-directed effort gradually created a network of sluices which enabled a great leap forward in agriculture. For some time, Madeira was a large grain producer.

In 1452, the first sugar mill was established. Four years later, Madeira's sugar was already being exported as far as England. Slowly, attracted by the prospect of good profits, a relatively-large number of foreign and Portuguese traders came to the island and settled down there. In 1451, Funchal and Machico, the two main villages on the island of Madeira, were raised to the status of *vila* (small town) and granted a royal charter *(foral)*.

The colonization of the Azores started much later and produced its first important results much later too. It was only in

1439 that a royal charter authorized Prince Henry to start the settlement, which actually began in the early 1440s. Like Madeira, the whole archipelago had been granted to Henry and to the Order of Christ.

In addition to Santa Maria and São Miguel, Terceira, Graciosa, Faial and Pico were populated and granted to captain-donataries. Captains and settlers were given privileges, lands and revenues in much the same way as in Madeira.

Wood and dyestuffs held first place in the economic development of the Azores for a while. Again, fish played a decisive role in local supply. Cattle and wheat would become the major sources of profit and export, but only after the 1470s. Sugar production never developed, because of the unfavourable climate; consequently, not many slaves were introduced in the archipelago.

The West African coast did not become profitable until the 1440s. The first black Africans were brought in 1441 and, from then on, the slave trade continued to flourish. While some captives came as a result of direct incursions inland by the Portuguese, most of them were regularly purchased from Muslim traders and black Africans themselves. A great number, the majority perhaps, were then profitably sold on to Castile, Aragon and other European countries, only a part being employed in the sugar plantations (as well as in other agricultural or domestic jobs) in Madeira and Portugal.

From Guinea, the Portuguese also imported gum arabic, civet cats, red pepper, cotton, ivory and several others minor items, including parrots. Other lucrative operations involved fish and oil traffic. In addition to fish, the Portuguese ships caught whales and sea wolves in the Canarian and North African waters, the skins and oil of which were then sold in Portugal and exported everywhere.

Gold, the much-coveted object, was first brought to Portugal in 1442. It was exchanged for wheat, which was in great demand by the Africans. This explains why the Portuguese, themselves always short of grain, often brought it from abroad or from Madeira, not for national consumption but for the purpose of obtaining gold. Cloth and clothes, blankets, red coral in the form of beads and silver were also demanded by the Africans and could be used as a means of exchange for gold. The intensity of traffic with the African coast, Prince Henry's monopoly, and the changes occurred in the Portuguese currency suggest that the amount of gold did play a significant role in the country's economy and in achieving the desired aims.

In 1443, Prince Henry succeeded in obtaining the monopoly of all the trade carried on with the African coast south of the Bojador. Trade monopoly did not signify navigation exclusivity. Private undertakings continued, although Henry's permission was now necessary. In this way, Henry's monopoly resembled any other lordship, similar to the seigniorial lands he held at home.

By the late-1440s, the first regular trading post was created in the island of Arguin (20.5° N), not far from the mainland. It was almost immediately rented out to a Portuguese company for ten years. In the 1450s, a second trading post (and probably a castle too) was founded some miles south of Arguin.

THE RENAISSANCE STATE

The end of Prince Pedro's regency brought about the last great epoch for the feudal aristocracy. Right until the end of his long reign (he died in 1481), Afonso V never gave up those two ideals which his uncles Afonso and Henry so perfectly represented: the constant strengthening of the noble houses to the detriment of the crown (a typical feudal point of view which caused the king to be praised, respected and beloved by his peers, the feudal lords), accompanied by a systematic policy of conquests in Morocco (which, again, the nobility welcomed as a means of displaying bravery, achieving fame and obtaining profits).

When Henry IV, king of Castile, died (1474), the feudal party, hostile to his sister Isabella (who, meanwhile, had married Ferdinand of Aragon and had proclaimed herself queen of Castile), offered the crown of the realm to the Portuguese monarch, provided he married Juana, daughter of the late king. Afonso proclaimed himself king of Castile and invaded the territory, but failed to decisively beat the enemy at Toro (1476). He returned to Portugal and tried to recruit French intervention from the north. He even decided to travel to France and personally convince King Louis XI of the justness if his cause, but in vain. Disillusioned, he returned to Portugal and included his son John more actively in the business of the crown. The treaty of Alcáçovas (1479) established peace, with the king of Portugal renouncing all his rights to the Castilian crown and obtaining, in exchange, several important concessions in Africa.

John II (1481-95), a typical Renaissance ruler, embarked on a dangerous fight against the great feudal lords. The upper nobility responded with a widespread conspiracy against the king, where Castilian involvement played a part. Aware of these links, John II struck back: the Duke of Bragança, the head of the conspiracy, was quickly tried and beheaded, while the other known or suspected leaders were forced to flee the country to save their lives. As a result, the king got rid of the strongest feudal family in the country, whose titles were abolished and whose huge properties suddenly enlarged the crown's estate. After the Braganças, the second feudal lord of the realm, the Duke of Viseu, cousin and brother-in-law to the king, became the obvious target. Foolish enough to lead a second conspiracy, he was stabbed by the king himself (1484), while his followers suffered death at the stake or fled to Castile.

The expulsion of the Jews from Castile and Aragon (1492) posed a serious problem for Portugal. Many Spanish Jews offered John II a considerable amount of money if he allowed them into the country. John II compromised: he authorized the Jews' admission at the price of eight cruzados each, but he refused to let them stay for longer than eight months. Once that deadline expired, a great number were reduced to captivity; only some 600 families succeeded in purchasing a permanent residence permit. As they were the wealthiest and the most powerful, their mere presence caused an inbalance in the state of harmonious coexistence with the Christians and led to ruthless measures over the following reign.

Manuel I (1495-1521) restored the Braganças and the other banished families full ownership of their former dignities, privileges and estates. Being the governor of the Order of Christ, and benefiting from the first profits from India, he could afford to be generous and merciful. For more than a century, and in spite of all their affluence and prestige, the Braganças (like all the other noble families) would pose no particular threat to the royal policy of authority and centralization. The same could be said of the Church.

A more difficult problem was presented by the Jewish question. Manuel freed the Jews reduced to captivity at the beginning of his reign. Yet, only a year later, he decided on their expulsion. Several thousands preferred to accept baptism. Known as New Christians *(cristãos-novos),* they were to be left in peace until 1534.

Manuel's other concern was Castile. After the medieval attempts and the campaigns of Afonso V, a peaceful but systematic succession of royal marriages was to be woven. The death of John, the heir to the Castilian-Aragonese throne, put Princess Isabel, Manuel's wife, in direct order of succession (1497). Two months later, however, Isabel died in labour, and their son, Miguel, became the heir to the three crowns, which would unify the Peninsula. But he died shortly after (1500). The dream was over.

In the meantime, Vasco da Gama had reached India by sea (1498), and his triumphal return to Portugal (1499), his ships loaded with spices, brought the king immense fame and prestige. Acclaimed as the richest monarch in all Christendom, he took on many new and grand titles. From 1500 onwards, and throughout his lifetime, the Portuguese obtained nothing but victories from Arabia to Malaysia, gaining control of the Indian Ocean.

The long reign of John III (1521-57) can be divided into two main periods, with differences occurring in the economic situation, religious attitude, cultural policy and even psychological mood of the sovereign. The tolerant Renaissance prince and patron gave away to a fanatic, narrow-minded ruler, entirely in the hands of the Jesuits and the defenders of a strict counter-Reformation policy, arresting and condemning the very same people he had formerly invited, niggardly cutting back funds and subsidies, closing schools and generally isolating himself and his country from any external influences.

John's external policy ran relatively smoothly, despite the increasing French attacks on Portuguese ships and Atlantic possessions. The king was becoming less and less interested in European affairs in general, absorbed as he was by the great overseas expansion. He reached an agreement on the Moluccas with his brother-in-law, Charles V, in 1529.

Portugal's expansion and apparent wealth made her respected by all the European kingdoms. John II, Manuel I and John III acquired a certain fame as good administrators and models of Renaissance princes. No wonder that international contacts became plentiful, and that cultural and economic interchange served the interests of all.

•

The country's demographic setting changed after 1450. Gradually, stagnation evolved into a steady increase in population. It seems that this new trend permeated the entire 16th century. In 1527-32, the first census in Portuguese history showed the existence of a minimum of 1 000 000 and a maximum of 1 500 000 persons. Lisbon, a great metropolis by European standards, and a huge city for Portugal, was home to between 50 000 and 65 000 inhabitants. Next came Porto, and then Évora and Santarém.

Between the ethnical minorities, the Jews formed a relatively-small group, organized in communes (*comunas*). They had their own synagogues, and had to live in separate quarters (*judiarias*), segregated from Christian areas by walls, fences and gates which had to be closed at night. The Moors were gradually reduced to a small group, because of continuous integration into the Christian community and migration to Muslim countries. They were organised in much the same way as the Jews.

The two main characteristics of Portuguese agriculture in the period from 1450 to 1550 were probably the resumption of land reclamation and the introduction of new cultures, particularly maize. Wine and oil production increased, while grain output remained stationary or even declined. The obvious result was the need for more imports. Maize, known in Portugal before 1525, quickly attracted Portuguese farmers, generally replacing the existing millet and often successfully supplanting wheat in its traditional areas.

The only important «industries» were shipbuilding and biscuit production. Both belonged to the crown. In shipbuilding, the Portuguese were constant innovators; they made significant improvements and became famous for the unrivalled quality of their ships.

The expansion overseas brought a new and decisive element in late-medieval Portuguese trade, namely the introduction of a great variety of exotic and expensive merchandise, unheard of or scarcely existing in Portugal before. This fact converted Portugal into an intermediary between Europe and Africa, and, later, Asia and America as well. Even so, salt, wine and fruit, along with cork, continued to be exported in significant amounts and bring prosperity to a large number of landowners and traders. The most famous and important of all Portuguese trade ports was the one in Flanders, set up firstly in Bruges and later moved to Antwerp. This trade port quickly became the herald for Portugal's new produce, introduced by the country's expansion overseas. Early in the 16th century, the bulk of the trade-port business consisted of spices brought from Africa and India.

As far as domestic trade was concerned, fairs became less relevant, whereas local markets tended to expand. In every town, the number of shops, their concentration and specialization increased and became more complex.

The abundance of gold gave birth to the famous Portuguese *cruzado*. Also, the discovery after 1450 of new technological processes in extracting silver led to the end of the silver shortage. Thus, the monetary reform of 1489 was successful and that explains the remarkably stable period that followed that year, the real beginning of a new era in the history of Portuguesecurrency.

The concentration of land in the hands of a few permeated the second half of the 14th and most of the 15th centuries. A schematic map of seigniorial Portugal clearly shows that, by the 1470s, the royal estate had been greatly reduced. Furthermore, and following the general European trend, a landslide of new titles (dukes, marquises, viscounts, barons) revealed royal preferences and favourites. To this upper nobility, a sort of «upper-middle nobility» should be added. They were all called royal vassals — *vassalos do rei* — and, as such, they were given a yearly fixed revenue *(contia)* by the crown which bore no relation to their estates.

Below these, another group of people were obliged to bear arms, although they were not entitled to any crown revenue. This group formed a sort of transition between the upper-middle aristocracy and the lower strata of the gentry *(fidalgos)*. The latter were more numerous, less wealthy in estates, less important in terms of top administrative and military offices, but more stable in their local influence and in maintaining the economic and social structures.

If John II succeeded in crushing the power of some of the most important noble families — namely the Braganças and his cousin Diogo —, and in substantially enlarging the royal patrimony at their expense, his successors Manuel I and John III were forced to step back and restore most of the confiscated estates to their former owners. However, the nobility of the early 16th century, if undiminished in privileges and revenues, showed a completely different stance, more in agreement with the policy of royal centralization. Firstly, they accepted their subordination to the king and his new absolutist state; secondly, in order to subsist, they became more and more dependent on royal appointments and temporary subsidies. As a consequence, a large part of the nobility migrated from their estates and local courts to the king's court and residence. At the same time, a great number of nobles indulged in commercial undertakings of all kinds, competing with the rising bourgeoisie and preventing its full development.

The structure of the clergy was less affected during this period. The union of the religious-military orders to the crown was perhaps the major significant event. Authorized to marry and to own private property, the military knights ceased to be churchmen, and knighthood became a simple mark of distinction.

The traditional tripartite division of society was breaking down and being replaced by a manifold and much more fluid classification which reflected the social transformation of the period. Class transition became easier, and important subdivisions in each of the three orders started playing a greater social role. Within the popular ranks, there were at least four major categories in the late-1400s and early-1500s: lawyers, citizens, artisans and all the others. The growing import of slaves introduced a new class of people, to whom all rights were denied. Conversion to Christianity might help but not necessarily account for enfranchisement.

For general administrative and judicial purposes, the kingdom of Portugal was divided into six provinces, also called *comarcas:* Entre-Douro-e-Minho, Trás-os-Montes, Beira, Estremadura, Entre-Tejo-e-Odiana (also called Alentejo) and the Algarve. In each of those large *comarcas,* the king was represented by a *corregedor,* whose powers in the judicial and administrative fields never ceased to develop. Besides the division into *comarcas,* the realm was divided, for financial purposes, into *almoxarifados,* each one under the authority of an *almoxarife,* who collected the crown revenue in his district. A third major division concerned mainly the Church, but was often used for civil purposes too: the bishoprics, with no change since the «Reconquista». According to the new demographic realities of the country, new bishoprics were created: Miranda do Douro, Leiria, Portalegre and Elvas.

Reforms in government and administration of justice, if not so conspicuous or revolutionary as in many other fields, nonetheless gave clear proof of the new trends in ruling the country. Within the main courts, the tendency was for greater centralization under stricter control by magistrates closer to the monarch. A new court created by John II, called *Mesa* or *Tribunal do Desembargo do Paço,* was especially focussed on petitions for pardon, privileges, freedom and legitimations. A second new court was the *Mesa da Consciência e Ordens* (Conscience and Orders Board), instituted in 1532. A third court was the *Holy Office of the Inquisition,* a successful attempt at royal interference in people's consciences. In government, the rising complexity and number of public affairs led to the creation of a veritable cabinet, composed of ministers or secretaries. The king was still assisted by a *state council.*

The role played by the *cortes* tended to become less and less relevant. Gradually, the king forgot the benefits of periodical dialogue with his people. Contact between the two ceased to be direct and tended to rely on bureaucracy alone.

Humanism in Portugal started later than in Castile, but earlier than in many other European countries. It began in Italy, and extensive relationships with the Italian city-states, particularly in the economic field, accounted for its quick import and development. Indirect influences arrived via France, the Netherlands, England or Spain, where a good many Portuguese were studying in the mid- and late-1400s.

Almost all secondary and university education experienced the humanist influence. At university level, in the many monastic and cathedral schools, in the newly-founded colleges and in private tutoring, the number of foreign-trained tutors and the quality of their teaching entirely renovated subjects and programs. Furthermore, the king invited a number of foreign scholars to occupy many of the teaching positions.

Around the same time, several new colleges were being founded in Portugal for young aristocrats or the rich bourgeoisie, thus initiating the modern boarding school system. The most famous was the one in Braga, founded by Clenardus, and the College of Arts and Humanities *(Colégio das Artes e Humanidades)* which followed the French model.

The university reform bore the imprint of the state and pertained to the great efforts of political centralization. John III undertook a complete cultural reform, with the final goal of getting rid of the feudal privileges of the University of Lisbon and founding a new and more docile school of high studies in Coimbra. Although the five great subjects — Theology, Canons, Law, Medicine and Arts, along with Mathematics — remained unaltered, the number of chairs within each one was considerably increased. Moreover, the new ordinances or bylaws granted to the University of Coimbra stressed its subordination to the royal authority and weakened its traditional relationship to the Pope and the Church. The university became an instrument of royal power.

The impact of humanism was not so clear in literature and general literary production. In history, the great chronicler Fernão Lopes was still a «medieval man» and combined the inevitable praise for the victors with a frank appraisal of events and human beings. His successors, Gomes Eanes de Zurara, Rui de Pina, João de Barros and Damião de Góis, less rustic and courtlier, as true Renaissance men, produced rather elaborate monuments of laudatory rhetoric and other formal gifts, notwithstanding an often invaluable description of facts and details.

Under conditions similar to the ones which had originated the poetry of the troubadours in earlier times, there arose, particularly in the courts of Afonso V and John II, a kind of light poetry, traditional in form and full of charm and spontaneity. Its verses were compiled by Garcia de Resende (1470?-1536) in the so-called *Cancioneiro Geral* («General Song-Book»). However, the outstanding representative of this late medieval flourishment was undoubtedly Gil Vicente (1465?-1537?), the creator of Portuguese theatre and a social critic.

It was only after 1520 that humanists reacted against what they considered to be old-fashioned themes and forms, their criticism broadly assailing Portugal's cultural milieu. Because of this late triumph of humanism in literary circles, the great names of the Portuguese Renaissance flourished only in the second half of the 16th century.

However, the key to understanding the rise and development of humanism in Portugal lies in the intensity of international contacts. Overseas expansion brought Portugal international publicity and contributed to her cultural development in an intense way. At the same time, an import of foreign scholars for teaching positions also aimed at preparing future generations' larger elite. Great names in the history of humanism were invited to come to Portugal — Erasmus, for one —, and even when they refused for whatever reason, they felt flattered and regarded Portugal sympathetically.

Contemporary to this great movement, and one of the main reasons for its upsurge, was the establishment of the printing press. The Portuguese press was implemented in 1488, by German initiative. In the 1500s, Portuguese book printing did increase, although with the predominance of works on theology and religion. Translations were also abundant, as might be expected in a small country like Portugal.

The classical period of Renaissance art in Europe displayed a highly-interesting complexity in Portugal. Four different «styles», albeit rarely displayed in a pure form, interacted and blended together with extreme originality in most monuments. These were the late-Gothic style, the so-called «Manueline», the *Mudéjar,* and, finally, the Renaissance styles. In painting, a great school of artists, or one great artist (Nuno Gonçalves) with several disciples, did flourish from the early 1470s to the end of the century. In the early 1500s, the schools of Lisbon and Viseu polarized painting, originating with a large and varied production of masterpieces. Both gradually absorbed the Italian influences that only after the 1540s or 1550s would prevail.

The contribution of Portugal to the Renaissance, however, was not so much in the arts or humanities, but rather in science navigation, astronomy, natural sciences, mathematics and, of course, geography. Furthermore, to a new knowledge of facts the Portuguese added a new method and a new approach, based on experience.

The Portuguese commenced their navigations and first contact with strange peoples and civilizations using medieval equipment and a general approach based on authority. Such an attitude prevailed for a long time. Universities, printed books and scholarly culture all continued to teach and accept the old masters with the old errors, long after everyone, from the humblest sailor to the noblest viceroy, had actually observed and experienced a different reality. For a long time, official learning and practical experience coexisted apparently without friction, yet often contradicting each other. However, the «revolution of experience» was definitely a revolution, and a subversive one. It was regarded as heretical, absurd and immoral. The Portuguese of the 15th and 16th centuries proved, by experience and scientific deduction: that the Atlantic Ocean was navigable and free from monsters; that the equatorial world was inhabitable and inhabited; that it was possible to sail systematically offshore and to become perfectly oriented by observing the sun and the stars; that Africa had a southern end and that there was a sea passage to India; that the pseudo-Indies discovered by Columbus were, in fact, a new continent separating Europe from East Asia, and that the three Americas formed a continuous land; that South America had a southern end too, and that there was a sea passage to India westward; that the three great oceans were connected; that the Earth was round and navigable all around. They mapped the contours of the continents and the oceans and, for the first time, sketched an ecumenical geography of the Earth. They drew the first map of the southern skies. They brought knowledge of many unknown civilizations and cultures to the western world, while putting many others into permanent contact. They faced and posed the problem of fusing, compromising or segregating often highly-complex cultures. They had to find a way of communicating in different languages with entirely new structures and writing signals. They tasted numerous new or insufficiently-known plants, fruits and foods, and brought them to Europe. They discovered and described new animals. The decisive steps in this immense world of experience took place before 1550, yet its full scientific description and significant impact on mankind lasted for centuries.

In Portugal, Reformation never existed as an organized movement. No real grievances existed against the moral condition of the clergy, who did not appear more corrupt or unrespected than previously. The «Reformists» or Reformation-oriented Portuguese were only a hundful of intellectuals, influenced less by direct meditation than by contact with foreigners. Furthermore, the establishment of the Inquisition promptly discouraged such tendencies by closing the country off to uncensored contact with the foreign world.

In fact, the Inquisition had little to do with the Reformation, at least as a real motive for its foundation. King Manuel had pleaded its establishment to the Pope as early as 1515, two years before Luther's rebellion. His real purpose was to secure one more resource to achieve centralization and royal control. The Inquisition was finally «bought» from Rome by John III (1536), but with great restrictions to full freedom of action. In the meantime, the first victims had been burned in Évora (1543).

THE RISE OF THE EMPIRE

By the early 1460s, the Portuguese had reached the Gulf of Guinea. From 1469 to 1474, the entire northern coastline of the Gulf of Guinea had been explored, along with the beginning of the eastern part of the Gulf. In 1474, the future John II was put in charge of overseas expansion. It is to him, rather than to Prince Henry, that the creation of a comprehensive plan of discovery, with both means and goals, should be credited. Yet the situation at home prevented resuming the discoveries before the early 1480s. With the Treaty of Alcáçovas (1479), Castile acknowledged the Portuguese monopoly to the south of the Canaries. North of these islands, the Portuguese were also recognized as masters in the Madeira and Azores archipelagos. In exchange, Portugal gave up her rights on the Canary Islands.

In 1482, John II sent his first expedition to Africa under the command of Diogo Cão, who discovered Gabon, Congo and most of Angola. On a second trip, he went as far as today's Namibia. In 1487, Bartolomeu Dias explored the coasts of Namibia and South Africa, sailed around the Cape of Good Hope and rightly concluded that he had finally reached the end of Africa and that the seaway to India was, at last, opened (1488).

Along with the discovery of Africa, the Portuguese also tried to navigate westward, searching for new islands. Before

1474, Greenland or Newfoundland were probably reached. In 1483 or 1484, Christopher Columbus, who had lived for several years in Lisbon and in Madeira, where he had learned the art of navigation and acquired geographical knowledge, proposed to King John II reaching India sailing westward. However, the Portuguese cosmographers rightly suspected that Diogo Cão had been closer to India than anyone else, and insisted on carrying on exploring eastward. Columbus's plan was dismissed, and the Genoese offered his services to Castile, where geographical knowledge was less developed than in Portugal.

When Columbus himself, returning from America after his first voyage (March 1493), called at Lisbon and paid a visit to the king, John II reminded him that the newly-discovered lands belonged to the Portuguese crown, for they lay south of the Canary Islands (treaty of 1479-80). Negotiations started immediately and, with the Treaty of Tordesillas (1494), the earth was divided into two areas of discovery and conquest according to a meridian line passing 370 leagues (1,184 miles) west of the Cape Verde islands. The western share would belong to Castile, the eastern to Portugal. Precise as it was, the 370 leagues detail clearly showed that the Portuguese monarch had some knowledge of lands somewhere in the Atlantic, lying west of the 100-league limit initially proposed by the Pope.

Vasco da Gama departed from Lisbon in July 1497, sailed around the Cape of Good Hope and, after having reached the limit of Bartolomeu Dias's navigations, began marking his own discoveries until Malindi (Melinde), a little further north of Mombasa (Kenya). There, he hired a famous Arab pilot who led the ships to India. After three months of negotiations, Vasco da Gama started on his way back home, his ships loaded with spices and other coveted merchandise. He arrived in Lisbon in 1499.

A new and much more robust expedition was immediately prepared, commanded by Pedro Álvares Cabral, in March 1300. The ships followed the same route as before but, for no apparent reason, they sailed more towards the south-west. This led them to the discovery of Brazil, on April 22, 1500. They landed north of present-day Porto Seguro (16° S), met the natives, and explored the coastline for a while. Cabral then proceeded to India, where he arrived in August 1500. Contemporary descriptions show that the discovery of Brazil caused no surprise. Whether Brazil had actually been reached before, perceived in the distance, or simply conjectured from some signs of land continues to be a matter for argument among historians.

Columbus's challenge stimulated other Portuguese expeditions westward, particularly in the northwest direction. By 1495, Pêro de Barcelos and João Fernandes Lavrador discovered or rediscovered Greenland. In 1500, Gaspar Corte Real reached Newfoundland, which he explored in detail. Later voyages discovered or explored some islands or even fragments of the mainland along the North-American coast.

In South America, several Portuguese expeditions searched the Brazilian coastline and reached what is now Uruguay and Argentina, up to the Rio de la Plata (River Plate) area. In south Atlantic waters, the few existing islands had all been discovered early in the 16th century.

South of the River Plate, the American continent definitely fell within the Spanish area, even by the often imprecise 16th century measurements. Yet it was again a Portuguese, Fernão de Magalhães (Magellan) who, for the first time, serving the Spanish king, reached most of present-day Argentina and Chile, and then crossed the Pacific Ocean. Magellan's intent was not so much to circumnavigate the world as to find a seaway to the

Moluccas, an important source of spices, while avoiding «Portuguese waters» as much as possible.

The Indian Ocean and the Asian continent were, by the same time, almost thoroughly «discovered» and «explored» from a Western point of view. Before the arrival of the Portuguese, no detailed maps of Asia were available to Europeans. This the Portuguese did first, with the help of partial Muslim portolan charts, publishing detailed voyage routes and sea charts of the entire Indian Ocean.

In the Pacific, the first Portuguese expedition arrived in 1511, after having explored most of present-day Indonesia, up to Timor. Shortly afterward, they may have reached, or seen, the north Australian coast. Jorge Álvares was the first Westerner to sail to China (1513). In the early 1540s, Japan was visited by Fernão Mendes Pinto.

The economic, political, and religious events and conditions that had forced the Portuguese out of Europe also promoted voyages of exploration inland, where a better knowledge of things and peoples might be obtained. Timbuktu was reached by them, as well as Mali. In the Congo region, they explored most of that kingdom and the northern part of Angola, to the south of it. In eastern Africa, Zimbabwe and the important kingdom of Monomotapa were visited. Official missions to Ethiopia were among the main concerns of the Portuguese. In Asia, countless expeditions took place, most of them undertaken by private merchants or peddlers looking for profits. Some of them became well-known thanks to written descriptions. Fernão Mendes Pinto visited southeast Asia, China and Japan, traveling extensively for about 17 years (1537-54). In Brazil, contacts with the hinterland began shortly after the discovery. The establishment of the captaincies favoured the exploration of the interior, generally in search of gold, precious stones and spices.

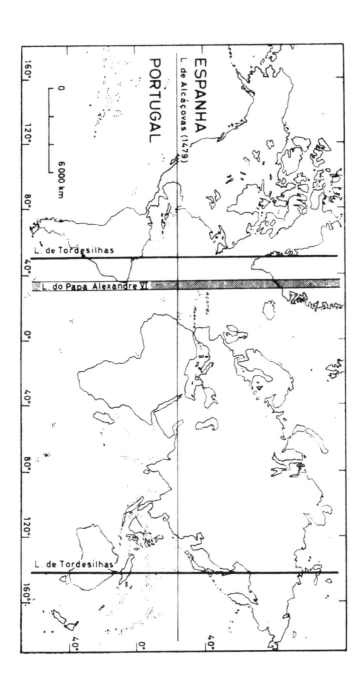

The Portuguese soon realized that, to secure control of spice sources and trade in the Indian Ocean, they had to destroy the long-established network of Muslim traders and trading places.

Sent by King Manuel as a viceroy *(vice-rei),* Francisco de Almeida arrived in India in 1505 with a definite program of political action. His instructions included the building of several fortresses at key strategic points, and the permanent stationing of a fleet in the Indian Ocean. He was expected to enforce the Portuguese monopoly of long-distance trade. His successor, Afonso de Albuquerque (1509-15), had a better knowledge of places and peoples. A more daring assessor of military forces and a much greater strategic genius, Albuquerque was both the true founder of the Portuguese «empire» in Asia and the best warrant of its permanence. In little more than six years, he anchored the Portuguese to the East Indian Ocean by conquering Malacca (1511) and so controlling all the maritime traffic with the Pacific; he imposed the Portuguese authority and sovereignty on Hormuz (Ormuz), thus controlling the Persian Gulf (1507 and 1515); and he established a territorial base for the seat of Portuguese administration by conquering Goa (1510). Albuquerque's main achievement was probably to have made the Portuguese the successors of Muslims in international Asian trade.

Albuquerque's successors were, as a rule, less famous than him and have been more accused of misdemeanours, cruelty and deeds of corruption. Yet Portuguese fortune was far from declining; rather it was rising and continued to do so until the middle of the 16th century. Colombo, in Ceylon, was taken in 1518, and the island became a pivotal piece in the Portuguese system. Other fortresses were built. In China, the Portuguese obtained Macao (1557) on a sort of permanent lease.

Openly defying the Muslim hegemony and combatting the Islamic faith, the Portuguese obtained privileges, concessions and alliances mainly among Hindu states. As their main enemies in Asia, they had to meet the Egyptians and the Turks, allied to the many smaller Mohamedan kingdoms. Most of the sea and land struggle took place in the western Indian Ocean, between Arabia and India.

•

The experimental laboratory for the Portuguese empire in Asia and America was in the North Atlantic: the Azores and Madeira islands and, later, Cape Verde and São Tomé.

By the second half of the 15th century, Madeira had become a small replica of metropolitan Portugal. It produced and exported sugar, its main source of wealth. The second economic activity was the production of wine, exported in large quantities.

The Azores rapidly became prosperous and economically useful to the mainland. In the late-1400s, wheat became the chief source of revenue, being exported in large quantities. Woad and *urzela (Litmus roccella)*, first-rate dyestuffs for the industrial countries of Europe, were also widely exported with good profits.

In the Cape Verde islands, effective colonization proved more difficult. Cultures considered essential in those days failed in Cape Verde. A permanent settlement required more effort and different forms of adjustment from the ones that the Portuguese were then prepared to make.

In the Gulf of Guinea, conditions were, again, different. Located on the equator, São Tomé, Príncipe, Ano Bom and Fernando Pó benefited from abundant and regular rainfall, coupled with highly-fertile soil. On the other hand, the hot climate, excessive humidity and numerous tropical diseases made for unhealthy living conditions that were hard to cope with and discouraged a permanent European settlement. Nonetheless, as in Cape Verde, the arrival of the first colonisers followed the islands' discovery by only a few years.

In continental Africa, settlement was intended only as a means of strengthening trade ports or supporting vital fortresses. In the northern hemisphere, besides Arguin, a group of well-fortified castles, all protecting small trading villages and towns, rose along the Gulf of Guinea. The «capital» of all these settlements (called «Mina» and the main source for the gold trade) was São Jorge da Mina (in present-day Ghana).

South of Guinea, the other African area of Portuguese expansion was the Congo. The Portuguese believed they were dealing with a more advanced culture and with more sophisticated and powerful rulers than they actually were. For more than a century, the Congo was a Portuguese protectorate in Africa and a great producer of slaves. As the slave demand continually increased, Congo's human resources were exhausted and traders were forced to look for them further south, in what is now Angola, with important gains in geographic knowledge of that country.

On the east African coast, settlement was understood in terms of trade relationships with the Indian Ocean. The Portuguese secured native permission to built fortresses in Sofala and Kilwa, as well as in the Island of Mozambique. Some trade ports were also established inland. Farther south, explorer Lourenço Marques contacted the local chieftains in the area where the present bay of Maputo is located and succeeded in setting up trade patterns and the basis for a permanent Portuguese establishment.

Colonization in India meant little more than strengthening and making permanent the cornerstones of Portuguese trade monopoly. Thus, governor Afonso de Albuquerque's policy of converting Goa into a European town and fostering mixed marriages of Portuguese and Hindus aimed only at strengthening Goa's position as the capital of a trade emporium. Comparable to Goa was only Malacca, the town the Portuguese promoted to their far-eastern capital. There, also, an intermarriage policy was fostered, and a caste of mixed-race people gradually emerged.

The crown representative in the Portuguese settlements from Sofala to Macao was the governor-general (sometimes promoted to viceroy — *vice-rei),* appointed by the king for a three-year period. He appointed local authorities, directed attack and defense campaigns, supervised the economic policies and was responsible for the maintenance and enforcement of law.

The Brazilian settlement developed slowly. In the first years after its discovery, Brazil yielded little more than brazil-wood, sugar cane and exotic animals. The crown rented out the trade monopoly, which brought wealth to its owners and drew attention to the new country. Clandestine Spanish and French fleets took their share in the profitable trade. The Portuguese crown decided to intervene, fostering colonization. The territory was thus divided into 15 captaincies *(capitanias)* of 50 leagues of coastline granted to a *capitão-donatário* whose powers were similar to those of the captains of Madeira, Azores and Cape Verde. Trade pertained both to the settlers, in a free system, and to the crown, which owned several monopolies. By the late-1540s, some two thousand Portuguese, aided by three or four thousand slaves, were permanently settled from Pernambuco to Santos. The Brazilian wood and sugar trade had reached unsuspected levels, competing with Madeira and São Tomé.

Slaves, gold and spices were the decisive trilogy in overseas trade. This trilogy continued to play a decisive role in the economic history of the Portuguese empire throughout the 16th century. The spice monopoly gave the crown a net profit of about 89 per cent, a rate that again explains India's appeal and the amazing efforts made by the Portuguese to control Asia's maritime commerce. Other items included ivory, leather and furs, musk, livestock and gum from Africa, and a huge variety of beautiful, rare or exotic merchandise from Asia. Sugar, which ranked between the latter items and the three main ones, often assumed a more important position than slaves.

State control made Lisbon the compulsory harbour for all overseas trade. Yet, Lisbon, like Portugal, was far from being the final destination of the traded merchandise as well as the origin of all the exports to Africa and India. The commercial routes connected Lisbon with a number of foreign markets, of which Antwerp (and, before that, Bruges) was far in the lead. Nor should the local Asian trade be forgotten, for the Portuguese replaced the Muslims in many respects, carrying on their initiatives and following their long-established routes.

By 1518-19, overseas trade represented 68 per cent of all of Portugal's resources, which meant that royalty and its institutions depended mostly on maritime expansion. Expenditures were also very high. From 1522 to 1551, the crown lost a yearly average of more than 100 thousand *cruzados* on wrecked or captured ships sailing between Lisbon and India or between Lisbon and Flanders.

•

For a small country, inhabited by less than two million people, the task of building an empire certainly appears immense. Yet, much more important than the size or the number of people was the presence of a strong royal authority; the consequent disengagement from internal political problems; the national cohesion necessary for common efforts; the economic, social and other pressures pointing toward expansion; and a number of local circumstances, which varied depending on the time and the country.

Secondly, Portugal never built a real empire requiring many armed men and extensive military force until the middle of the 16th century. From Brazil to the Moluccas, fewer than 40 thousand Portuguese were enough to enforce the economic blockade, protect the trade ports and man the fortresses; intimidate and punish rebels against their supremacy; and colonize four archipelagos and a long strip of coastline in a new continent. A much graver problem arose from the lack of *qualified* manpower, which became a real handicap by the second half of the 16th century. At the same time, numerous able Portuguese were forced to leave Portugal for economic, religious, political and personal reasons.

Another problem arose from the economic and social background of Portuguese people. The backbone of commercial empires like those of Venice, Genoa and, later, Holland had always been the existence of a strong middle-class of enterprising bourgeois. Portugal's middle-class was insufficient in both number and strength. The Portuguese expansion was essentially a state enterprise, to which private interests or initiatives were not indifferent. However, problems arose when the crown was tempted to substitute a purely mercantile policy for imperialism and sheer political domination, which required expenses disproportionate to possible profits. Moreover, the crown had a feudal structure based upon privilege that allowed the nobility and the Church to siphon off a good share of the profits for themselves without reinvesting them profitably. With a considerable part of the overseas production in foreign hands, it is easy to understand that the Portuguese would become transporters for others rather than for themselves.

Race, civilization and religion posed infinite problems. From Morocco to China, the Portuguese met with people of all races, cultural stages and beliefs.

In India, as elsewhere in the East, religion first appeared as a confusing issue. At first, the Portuguese thought that Hindus were Christians. However, they soon realized their error and started bringing with them more priests and more monks than were usually required. Both Brahmans and Buddhists were attracted to the Christian religion, not because it denoted any spiritual superiority but because it was new and active, vehemently preached, and highly appealing to the lower classes and castes. Yet it did not take long for the Asians to realize that Christianity stood for as much oppression and discrimination as their former beliefs. Thus, to enforce conversions, the Portuguese had to enforce discriminatory legislations against non-Christians.

Missionaries also realized they had to study the language and customs of the natives. Therefore, the best accounts of Asian cultures in the 16th century were made by the clerics. As a rule, missionaries were the ones to realize how complex the Asian cultures were and how deep the contradiction between these cultures and their own was.

The degree of racial prejudice depended very much on colour and culture. There was a whole gradation of race acceptance, starting with white Muslims or white Hindus and ending with very dark Africans or cannibal Amerindians. The establishment of the Inquisition, and the general hardening of Portuguese policies both at home and throughout the empire after the mid-1500s clearly introduced a stricter ethnical barrier than before.

The discovery of the Atlantic Ocean, particularly after the passage of the equator, posed a certain number of problems, all difficult to solve. The wind system south of the equator followed a symmetrical pattern to the one north of it, something the Portuguese realized around the 1480s, if not before. Such a discovery enabled them to prepare carefully the best route to and from Asia. Once in the Indian Ocean, the way to and from India was determined by the monsoon system. This enabled the Portuguese to time the arrival and departure of their fleets according to a very regular schedule.

Another problem resulted from the need for more and more off-shore travels. It took the Portuguese some time to make use of the skies as a practicable means of determining latitude. Using the wooden quadrant *(quadrante)*, the sextant *(balestilha)*, and, above all, the astrolabe *(astrolábio)*, which they developed and perfected, Portuguese pilots were able to figure out their position at sea with relative precision, although they never succeeded in discovering a satisfactory way of calculating longitude.

Late in the 1400s, the Portuguese also developed navigation guides *(roteiros)*, where the coastline and its adjacent waters were carefully described. *Roteiros* were used along with the so-called *livros de marinharia* («sailing books»), a type of handbook containing everything that a pilot should know.

When the equator was crossed, there was a further problem, that of determining a new star, or constellation, which might replace the now invisible North Star. The latitude of the sun in the southern hemisphere also required calculations which could not be found in the existing latitude tables. Gradually, the Portuguese discovered the advantages of the Southern Cross constellation as a substitute for the vanished North Star.

APOGEE AND DECLINE

Up until the 15th century, Castile had always been the leading party in striving for a united Iberia under her direct sovereignty. Later, however, both Portugal and Aragon played a role too. This explains the intermarriages that resulted in the thwarted attempts of 1474-79 and 1496-1500. During the 16th century, dynastic ties between the Portuguese and the Spanish royal families developed with such insistence and closeness that final union was the inevitable result.

However, the Iberian Union was not simply the whim of a small group of royals: it also became economically, socially and culturally viable. Indeed, from the middle of the 16th century onwards, the Portuguese empire and its general economic organization formed a sort of complement to the Spanish empire. At the same time, the direct economic relations between Portugal and Spain were becoming more interdependent. Spaniards and Portuguese also had common enemies, in growing numbers and activities: the French, the English and, later, the Dutch. Culturally, too, an Iberian union would simply consolidate the increasing process of «Castilianisation» which Portugal had been undergoing for a long time.

John III was succeeded by his grandson Sebastian. But Sebastian's young age required a regency: first by his grandmother,

Catarina, and then by his great-uncle Henry, the cardinal archbishop of Lisbon and inquisitor-general.

At the age of fourteen, Sebastian took over control of government. Sick in body and in mind, he cared little for governing and became rather lost in his dreams of conquest and expansion of the faith. Conquering Morocco was his primary ambition. But an army could not leave Portugal before the summer of 1578 and, even so, it was in a pitiful state of indiscipline and disorganization. Landing in Arzila, the army proceeded south under the king's personal command. Near El-Ksar-el-Kebir (Alcácer-Quibir), the Portuguese forces were completely defeated by Sultan Mulay Abd-al-Malik's army in the most disastrous battle in Portuguese history. Sebastian was killed and with him the cream of the country's nobility and men-of-arms.

Sebastian's death opened the way to the Iberian Union. Cardinal Henry succeeded to the throne, but he was an old gentleman of sixty-six, broken in health and in energy. Thus, several candidates claimed their right to the Portuguese crown: António, prior of Crato, illegitimate son of Luis, brother of John III; Catarina, daughter of Duarte (also John III's brother) and married to the Duke of Bragança, João; and Philip II, King of Spain, Manuel I's grandson.

Most of the people supported António, because they rejected the idea of a Spanish king and the prior of Crato was the only candidate brave enough to defy the might of Philip II. The Duke of Bragança, though supported by a great many noblemen and churchmen, acted very prudently, unwilling to sacrifice his opulent house to the hazards of a dubious political game.

It did not take Philip II long to gain the support of the upper clergy, most of the nobility, the intellectuals and bureaucrats, and the merchants. Even the dukes of Bragança were forced to submit and accepted Philip's candidacy. Late in June

1580, the Duke of Alba invaded Portugal with a strong army. Meanwhile, António had proclaimed himself king in Lisbon, Santarém, Setúbal and other places. A military march took the Spanish army to the Tagus in a few weeks. The Duke of Alba landed in Cascais, easily defeated António's improvised army at Alcântara and entered Lisbon that same day. The rest of the country was pacified in a couple of months. Philip arrived in Portugal early in December, decided to fix his residence in Lisbon for some time (1581-83), and summoned the *cortes* at Tomar (April 1581), where he was solemnly sworn in and acclaimed King of Portugal, under the title of Philip I. António tried his best to continue the fight with the help of France and England. The Azores alone sustained his flag of independence for three years.

An Iberian Union did not mean loss of identity for Portugal. Twenty-five chapters signed by the king at the *cortes* of Tomar provided a great deal of autonomy for the country, despite the fact that foreign policy now became common to Portugal and Spain. Administration remained entirely in the hands of the Portuguese. Advantageous innovations included the suppression of customs at the border, a favourable situation for Portugal in the export of wheat from Castile, and the grant of a loan for immediate expenses, partly used for redeeming captives in Morocco. The Portuguese were also allowed to travel to and within the Spanish empire.

After more than ten years of governmental chaos, misdemeanours and increasing taxation, the new patterns of administration, which seem to have been sufficiently enforced, along with the wise decision of maintaining Portugal's identity, explain the relative calm that prevailed. Prosperity returned and the empire was kept undisturbed. If grievances against Spain continued to exist, and if the yearning for a Portuguese king never ceased, there is no doubt that Philip's excellent administration (with few political persecutions) coped with the problem for a long time.

To Philip II succeeded (1598) his son Philip III (known as Philip II of Portugal) who entrusted power to favourites. The new policy from Madrid tended towards centralized administration, gradually reducing the autonomy of the various political units that made up the Spanish monarchy. It was the inevitable result of impending hard times which hovered over the Iberian kingdom. Very unpopular measures were taken, in violation of the 1581 chapters. After 1611, taxation increased in the form of compulsory loans. The signing of a twelve-year truce with Holland brought peace to the country and her menaced overseas territories, and enhanced her economic prosperity by opening the ports to the Dutch trade (1609). To appease discontent, the king decided to visit Portugal, where he spent some five months of the year 1619.

Yet the Spanish administration became increasingly unpopular in Portugal and a new element of resistance was gradually embraced by a large part of the population: *Sebastianism*. In its late-16th and early-17th century form, Sebastianism was simply the belief that King Sebastian had not died at Alcácer-Quibir and would soon return to claim his rightful throne. Several impostors rose now and then, claiming they were Sebastian who had come to redeem Portugal.

Instead of simmering down, the rumour acquired more and more adherents and became increasingly complex in its formulation. The prophecies of a certain Bandarra, a shoemaker who lived in John III's times and who heralded the future coming of a veiled (*encoberto*) king, redeemer of mankind, were now interpreted as referring to Sebastian and his fate. By the 1620s and 1630s, most people started merging the veiled Sebastian with some more visible body, who was none other than the Duke of Bragança, his lawful heir. Thus, Sebastianism evolved into strict patriotism, and Sebastianists identified themselves with the opponents of the Iberian Union.

Philip III died in 1621. His son and successor, Philip IV, entrusted the premiership to the count-duke of Olivares. Realizing the decline of Spain, the new prime-minister attempted a vast plan of reforms, all aimed at strengthening the country's position abroad and enforcing centralization at home. In the government of Portugal, Olivares implemented several measures to correct abuses, all very unpopular.

Overseas, the Dutch (and the English also) began their systematic attacks on the Portuguese vital centres. The Portuguese tended to blame the Spanish administration for everything that happened and to rely on Madrid for defence while, at the same time, objecting to increases in taxation and to the necessary army reforms. Such reforms aimed at unifying the local armies of the various units within the Spanish monarchy. In 1638 and 1639, cavalry and infantry forces were recruited in unprecedented numbers. Paid for with Portuguese money, these troops were destined by Olivares for combat somewhere in Europe, where the Portuguese thought their interests were non-existent. Also, a great number of noblemen and clerics were called to Madrid, ostensibly to discuss a new administrative reform. Presumably, Olivares's intent was to deprive Portugal of qualified leadership in case of an open rebellion. To increase the malaise, the New Christians were again given the opportunity to freely dispose of their wealth and to leave the country if they wished to, provided they paid the treasury the huge contribution of 1 500 000 cruzados.

•

There is little doubt that a spirit of nationalism was behind the restoration of Portugal's total independence after 60 years of dual monarchy. To the majority of the Portuguese, and particularly to the popular masses, the Spanish monarchs were nothing but usurpers, the Spaniards enemies, and their partisans sheer traitors. The gradual loss of cultural individuality was felt by many Portuguese and resulted in several reactions in favour of the Portuguese language and its expression by means of prose and poetry.

From an economic standpoint, the situation had greatly deteriorated since the 1620s, or even before. Many of the reasons that had justified the union of the two crowns became obsolete with the changing economic conjuncture. The whole Portuguese empire was going through a serious crisis with the victorious attacks of the Dutch and the English. The Cape route, axis of the economic structure, ceased to be the main source of prosperity and revenue. Instead, Portuguese trade between Lisbon and India was reduced to less than one-third after 1580. The Portuguese had lost their trade monopoly, which meant that everybody's revenues went down. Even the Atlantic-based trade declined with successive foreign attacks. Also, the Spaniards began to object strongly to sharing their empire with the Portuguese. This reaction aroused national feelings in Portugal as well as in Spain, widening the gulf between the two countries.

In Portugal, the economic situation was far from brilliant. Producers suffered with the fall in prices. The crisis affected the lower classes, whose poverty clearly increased, as in many other countries in Europe. Rising taxation made things harder still. At this time, people were rioting in several places, particularly in Alentejo (Évora) and the Algarve (1637). In June 1640, Catalonia revolted too. It is safe to say that without the Catalan uprising, Portugal's chances of seceding would have been minimal.

In November 1640, a conspiracy among the aristocrats obtained the Duke of Bragança's support. On December 1, a group of nobles attacked the royal palace in Lisbon and acclaimed the Duke as John IV. Almost everywhere in Portugal and throughout the empire overseas, the news of the change and the oath of allegiance required were well received and obeyed with little question. Only Ceuta remained faithful to the cause of Philip IV.

As in 1580, the Portuguese in 1640 were far from united. If the lower classes kept their nationalist faith intact and stuck with John IV, upper and lower nobles, often with family ties in Spain, hesitated, and only a portion definitely sided with the former Duke of Bragança. Most bureaucrats sided with John IV. As for the bourgeoisie, the great majority had no part in the secession movement and generally remained in neutral expectation. The clergy was also divided. The Jesuits supported John IV, a factor of primary importance, both for the national cause and for their own future prestige and power. The other orders were not so sure. And the Inquisition remained favourable to Spain, an understandable position if one recalls that the Inquisition had practically governed Portugal during the Iberian Union.

All things considered, the new king of Portugal was certainly not to be envied. His whole reign (1640-56) witnessed disaster after disaster for the Portuguese empire, a succession of diplomatic failures in Europe, and a poor economic situation at home, relieved only by a number of military achievements in Portugal that prevented widespread invasion. Within the country, several conspiracies were discovered, showing some discontent. The war mobilized all the efforts Portugal could spare and absorbed huge sums of money. Worse than that, it prevented the government from sending help to the often-attacked overseas possessions.

Portugal lacked a modern army and her fortifications were poor. From the Portuguese side, this explains why the war was generally confined to limited border operations. From the Spanish side, the Thirty Years' War (which lasted until 1659 in Spain) and the Catalonian affair (until 1652) delayed any major offensive. The rebellion of the Duke of Medina Sidonia, who, in 1641, tried to wrest Andalucía from Spain, diverted more troops from the Portuguese border. Some field battles brought victory to the Portuguese armies (Montijo, 1644; Linhas de Elvas, 1659); but, as a rule, the war had its ups and downs for both contenders.

John IV died in 1656. The new king, Afonso VI, a minor, was physically and mentally unfit for govern. A regency under Queen-Mother Luisa of Guzmán should have ended in 1657, but was indefinitely prolonged. This situation favoured the nobles — particularly a conservative group of nobles — who increased their power considerably.

A succession of disasters and failures occurred in the years that followed. In 1657, the Dutch attacked the Portuguese mainland and blockaded Lisbon for three months. In 1659, Portugal did not succeed in being accepted at the negotiations which led to the Treaty of the Pyrenees between Spain, the Empire, and France. As a consequence, a treaty in 1661 with Holland and the marriage of Princess Catarina to Charles II of England meant the subservience of the Portuguese interests to those of the other two powers in order to achieve peace and alliances.

Then, the great Spanish offensives started in 1661 and lasted until 1665. This brought about a growing opposition to Queen-Mother Luisa and her ruling *clique:* in 1662, a palace *coup d'état* transferred personal power to the king and installed a small group of younger and ambitious nobles. The Count of Castelo Melhor became prime minister. A new military effort, under better leadership and a more efficient government, brought about a series of victories for the Portuguese armies. Mercenaries came in considerable numbers. Moreover, Spain was tired of wars and nearly exhausted, while the Portuguese fought for their survival as a nation. Each Spanish offensive was stopped. The decisive battle of Montes Claros (1665) put an end to the war for all practical purposes.

To ensure succession to the throne and thus neutralize his enemies, Castelo Melhor married Afonso VI to a French princess, Marie Françoise of Nemours, better known as Mademoiselle d'Aumale (1666). But Afonso VI proved incapable of behaving like a husband, continuing to surround himself with the scum of society, running about the streets at night, and acting like a brigand and even a murderer.

In September 1667, a second *coup d'état* led by Prince Peter, brother of Afonso VI, forced the dismissal of Castelo Melhor and his partisans and eventually caused the imprisonment of the king himself. Peter took on the title of Prince Regent, restored the nobles as a class to their former power, and married Marie Françoise (1668) after Afonso's impotence had been proven in a scandalous inquiry.

The conditions for peace were now fulfilled. In Spain, Philip IV died in 1665, his son Charles II being a child of only four. The peace treaty was signed in 1668: it conferred full independence to Portugal and kept her borders unchanged. Only Ceuta remained in Spanish hands.

•

The great demographic push continued in the Iberian Peninsula at least until the end of the 16th century. Stagnation, if not actual decline, followed. Data points to a population of nearly two million people around 1640. Lisbon, with a maximum population of 165 thousand by 1620, could be compared to Venice and Amsterdam, huge cities for the time. The other Portuguese urban centres were much smaller: Porto, Coimbra, Évora and Elvas all had about the same population, between 16 and 20 thousand.

In agriculture, land reclamation continued. Maize often replaced wheat and rye as nourishment and made up for food shortages. The area devoted to cultivating wheat declined or stagnated. As a consequence, Portugal's dependence on foreign wheat became a constant factor. Wine became better and better known abroad. After 1650, English firms settled in Porto and began fostering wine production and export.

However, the main source of Portugal's revenue came from overseas. The spice demand gradually declined. Instead, shellac, china and other items from the Far East, along with sugar, wood and, later, tobacco from Brazil and the Atlantic Islands, rose to the top of the list of imports.

The dual union with Spain connected the Portuguese economic world to the Spanish. But the Restoration of 1640 brought no great advantages to external trade. War and foreign attacks on the Portuguese empire and Portuguese ships deterred long-distance trade. The profitable land traffic with Spain disappeared altogether. The Mediterranean was closed off to Portuguese traders.

The government of Portugal succeeded in fostering trade relations with northern Europe. However, the leading fact in Portugal's external trade after 1640 was its gradual surrender to English interests. The treaties with England gave this country freedom to trade with the Portuguese empire and special privileges to English residents in Portugal. The political alliance which ratified the treaty of 1661 (the marriage of Princess Catarina to Charles II) helped to promote England to the number one position in trade relations with Portugal.

Accepting the principle of an increasing royal centralization, the nobles were kept in most offices of command and became the instruments of top administration. When the independence of Portugal was again proclaimed in 1640, the choice of the Duke of Bragança as king, «elected» by his peers, gave strength to the aristocracy. The Bragancas never freed themselves from its influence. In 1670, when peace and prosperity returned to Portugal, power was being shared equally between the king and the aristocracy.

As a result of the Catholic «Reformation», a new ecclesiastical order gradually emerged, more independent and more conscious of itself than ever before, less participatory in the economic and social elements of the other classes. If the great majority of bishops and important abbots continued to come from a small number of lineages, recruitment in the upper ranks seems to have been somewhat more democratic. Within the lower ranks, the change was apparently in the opposite direction: ordination was limited to those who owned some patrimony or were given ecclesiastical benefits.

The great order of the late 16th and 17th centuries was unquestionably that of the Jesuits. They arrived in Portugal in 1540. They were 650 by the middle of the century. They owned a university and several important colleges. Their priests swarmed throughout Portugal and overseas and were among the most popular. Their main target was the youth, and in Portugal they almost succeeded in monopolizing regular education. For almost a century, they were good allies of the Inquisition and the secular clergy. Things started changing little by little as their power and wealth increased. After the 1620s, a hidden struggle opposed Jesuits and the Inquisition. They chose the cause of independence and were among the chief supporters of John IV.

Yet neither Protestants nor Jews posed a serious menace to the religious unity of the country. Consequently, the Portuguese Inquisition had to find a permanent target in order to justify its own existence. The New Christians were sufficiently numerous to provide a good one. By discriminating against them and accusing them of Judaism, the Inquisition created a true ghetto and kept it alive, instead of extinguishing it. The New Christians formed, in the main, a middle class of merchants and capitalists, and they were not well accepted by the small «Old Christian» Portuguese bourgeoisie, nor by the feudal nobility, nor by the poorer masses who regarded them as the descendants of the much-hated Jew usurers. A true state within the state, the Inquisition burned, from 1543 to 1684, at least 1 379 people at the *autos da fé* («acts of the faith»), an average of almost ten people a year. The total number of condemnations rose to a minimum of 19 247 in the same period, more than 136 each year. Hundreds of people also died in prison, where they were often kept indefinitely without trial.

The expansion of long-distance trade favoured the growth of a Portuguese merchant class, which probably reached its peak in the mid-1500s. But foreign traders came to Portugal in larger and larger numbers, attracted by good profits and royal privileges. The most profitable undertakings always belonged to the crown, the nobles or the foreigners. The Portuguese funded little and were not used to reinvesting at a rapid pace. They got no help from the state, and the numerous petty bourgeois were another obstacle. They were afraid of powerful trusts or big companies which might absorb or destroy them.

The dual union with Spain was favourable to a Portuguese bourgeoisie. The Madrid government was much more conscious of the importance of a middle-class in the structure of the realm. The New Christians enjoyed some periods of ease and prosperity. But the revolution of 1640 brought about a period of decline for the Portuguese bourgeoisie. Many foreigners settled down in Lisbon. They inflicted a deadly blow on Portuguese traders. The Inquisition acted freely and ruined a large number of firms and individual businessmen, preventing joint initiatives between Portuguese living in Portugal and Portuguese exiles abroad.

Artisans of most crafts remained gathered together in corporations, and so they were kept firmly «in their place». At *cortes,* many of the people's deputies belonged to the nobility. In the municipal government of Lisbon, most of the important administrative jobs were reserved for the aristocrats.

The number of slaves declined. At the same time, their process of integration speeded up, mostly through miscegenation. Several royal decrees forbade or made it difficult to import slaves to Portugal, particularly from India. Despite all this, a few thousand still lived in Portugal by the middle of the 17th century.

In the late 16th and 17th centuries, government by councils was developed, small bodies of people chosen from the ranks of the nobility, the clergy, and the bureaucrats. They advised the king and his ministers on affairs of importance. Later, after the restoration of independence, they limited and controlled royal power, often seizing power themselves. From 1662 to 1667, the *escrivão da puridade* was revived by the Count of Castelo Melhor as a true prime-minister, an intermediary between the king and his secretaries. The role of the *cortes* very much declined in favour of royal centralization. After the Restoration, their role was for a while somewhat enhanced, but afterwards they declined again.

The University became a state institution under the jurisdiction of the royal tribunal known as *Mesa da Consciência e Ordens*. The Coimbra monopoly in university courses was threatened by the Jesuits, who founded a new university in Évora. They also defended that admission into Faculties of Canons and Law should depend on a degree by the College of Arts, which they directed. The Jesuits, the Inquisition and the crown were at that time strongly united against heresy, cultural bourgeoning and deviations from the Council of Trent policy. Throughout the country, a great many teachers were persecuted, arrested, condemned or forced to leave their chairs. Few innovations in teaching and learning were ever accepted. Universities and colleges became very rigidified, rejecting the cultural advancement which was taking place elsewhere. Fruitful and progressive science rose only from the humble and pragmatic achievements of navigators, settlers overseas, travellers and foreigners.

Control of culture by the Church and the state was enforced through the introduction of organized censorship. From 1540 onwards, all bookstores were periodically inspected by ecclesiastics, as were ships coming from abroad. Works banned by the *Index Librorum Prohibitorum* included books considered heretical; books on «lascivious and dishonest things»; books on witchcraft, astrology, and the like. The formula later adopted by the censors forbade all books or part of books that contained anything against «our holy Faith and good customs». Writers like Camões, Gil Vicente, Sá de Miranda, António Ferreira, Bernardim Ribeiro, João de Barros and many others all had many of their works proscribed or mutilated by censorship.

Both the bishops and the king retained their power over literary production as well. All manuscripts due for publication were first presented to the Inquisition, then to the «Ordinary» (the bishop of the diocese), and finally to the king through the *Desembargo do Paço*. The final edition bore the permission of those three authorities. Censorship varied according to the times, the personality of the censors, and the influences backing the authors. In any case, it was always a discouraging element for writers and printers. Along with the Inquisition and the pervasive Jesuit influence, it slowed down literary production and prevented Portugal from accompanying the scientific and cultural progress of Europe at a normal pace.

Despite all these barriers to a full cultural development, the Portuguese world in the second half of the 16th and first half of the 17th centuries was still vigorous enough to produce a great number of masterworks and keep up with the cultural (if not scientific) advancements of Europe. The humanist revival yielded some of its best fruits after 1550: Luís de Camões, António Ferreira, Francisco de Holanda and, later, Diogo Couto, Luís de Sousa, Francisco Rodrigues Lobo, Francisco Manuel de Melo, António das Chagas and António Vieira. Yet there is little doubt that both number and quality (with the exception of Vieira) somewhat declined in the 17th century.

In the arts, the style of the Renaissance evolved to that new way of understanding the classical models, known as Mannerism. Italian and Spanish masters were eagerly copied everywhere. Inside churches, a lavish type of decoration developed that included both tiles *(azulejos)* and giltwood. This brought about several results, one of them being the decline of religious painting. Public buildings also became more and more numerous, their artistic expression gaining increasing value: military fortresses, aqueducts, palaces, noble farms *(quintas)*, fountains, schools, hospitals, etc.

THE TRIDIMENSIONAL EMPIRE

The history of the Portuguese empire in Asia from de mid-1500s to the 1630s was one of remarkable stability. There were few conquests but also few losses. Damão, annexed in 1559, concluded the period of expansion. The only important defeat was the loss of Hormuz (1622) to the Persians, helped by the English. Yet a chain of 11 fortresses still protected the Portuguese interests in the waters of the Persian Gulf.

But if the territorial «empire» was kept intact all those years, it would be wrong to suppose that nothing else had changed. Both the Dutch and the English had forced their way into the Indian Ocean, and the Portuguese could no longer claim full control of the sea traffic as before. Attacks on Dutch vessels started by 1603, fierce combat lasting for six years, when the truce of 1609 between Spain and Holland allowed the Dutch to trade freely in the Indian Ocean. The British entered the Indian Ocean in 1602, but instead of focusing their attention on the Far East, they dared to challenge the Portuguese at the very heart of their empire, India and Persia. By a clever system of alliances, they egged on local people against the Portuguese, helping them with weapons, ammunition, technicians, etc. Such alliances were able to defeat the Portuguese in some places, particularly in Arabia and Persia. However, up until the

1640s, the Portuguese were still the leading power in the Indian Ocean. If the Dutch and the English were firmly settled down in the Asian world by the 1630s and 1640s, it was more because there seemed to be room for everybody than because the Portuguese had been beaten and replaced.

The increased number of attacks and the lack of reinforcements from Europe explain the great Portuguese losses after 1630. Most of Ceylon was lost to the Dutch. After the Restoration of 1640, the losses were more frequent because the government had to organize resistance at home and could hardly send any reinforcements. By 1665, the empire in Asia had been reduced to Goa, Damão, Diu, Bassein, and a few unimportant fortresses in India; to Macao, in China; and to half of Timor, in Indonesia.

In East Africa, the Portuguese kept a line of fortresses and trade ports, coupled with some areas of influence, which extended from Lourenço Marques to Ethiopia. The trade accounted for the setting up of trade ports in Lourenço Marques (Delagoa Bay) in the late-16th and early-17th centuries. Mid-century, the various Portuguese possessions north of Cape Delgado fell one by one to the Arabs of Oman, helped by the British: only Mombasa resisted until 1698.

The number of Portuguese living in Asia and East Africa kept on increasing until the 1620s or 1630s, and then started to decline rapidly. Goa reached its demographic peak early in the 17th century, when it was equal to, or even surpassed, Lisbon in the number of people. But its population gradually declined and, by the 1630s, it was reduced to half or even less.

Though the Lisbon government officially decreed that the only bar to Portuguese citizenship should be religion, this policy was not implemented throughout Portuguese Asia. Even within the church, Asian Christians were not treated as equals.

The secular Church accepted them as priests but generally thwarted their move up the hierarchy. Nevertheless, the number of mixed-race people constantly increased due to the lack of European women. Slaves, of course, were abundant — of black, Muslim or Indonesian origin.

The viceroy or governor-general in Goa ruled the vast Portuguese Empire and areas of influence from East Africa to Japan. In the 1570s, the government of Portuguese Asia was subdivided into three large areas: one from East Africa to Ceylon, directly administered by the viceroy of India; the second from Ceylon to Pegu (present-day Burma); and the third from Pegu to China, each one controlled by a governor, subject to the supreme authority of the viceroy. Local administration belonged either to the municipal councils or to agents of the central government. Most trade ports and fortress cities were only subject to a sort of military government, with its officers appointed by the viceroy. Besides the network of cities, fortresses and trade ports, the Portuguese empire in Asia still depended on the government-organized fleets and navigation lines between the main ports. The most important line was the one that connected Portugal with Goa *(carreira da Índia)*.

The trade monopoly with the East had been firmly held by the state for more than half a century. Afterwards, there were successive periods with varying characteristics: contracts with individuals, freedom of trade, monopoly conceded to just one group and traditional state monopoly. In 1642, freedom of trade was definitively established with the exception of cinnamon, which remained in royal hands. The spice trade considerably declined after the mid-1500s. But cinnamon increased and became the main spice instead of pepper. Other merchandise supplemented the spice cargoes and gradually made up for them in preserving the profitability of the trips do India: pearls and

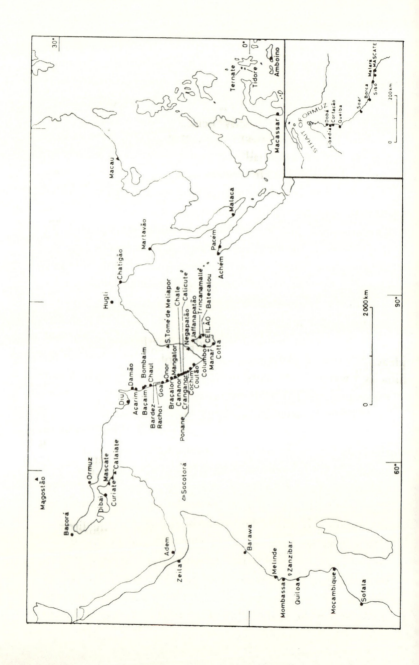

gems, diamonds, silk, cotton cloth, indigo, china, expensive furniture, etc.

The Portuguese traffic with Asia suffered two great crises which reduced its importance: one around 1591, when the amount and profit went down one-third; the other around 1650-60, which brought the Asian empire to an end. It is interesting to note that, in spite of all the competition by other countries, Portugal remained the main entrepot for spices and diamonds for most of Europe until about 1650.

With the coming of the Jesuits to Asia, a vast movement of religious expansion was launched. The spread of Christianity in the East made up for the stagnation in military conquests and represented a second phase in the history of the Portuguese empire. The Jesuits penetrated deeply into lands of diverse beliefs. Their methods were clever and efficient, their enthusiasm stirring, their capacity to endure hardships (including martyrdom) astonishing. Within half a century, their missions were everywhere, from Mozambique to Japan, reaching central and northern India, and most of China, as far as distant Tibet. By 1623, the Jesuit organization in the East comprised four «provinces»: Goa, Malabar, China and Japan.

Conversions were achieved quite rapidly and convinced many people in Europe that in a few years all of Asia would be Christian. However, the conversions were generally superficial, without any deep change in the traditional beliefs of Hindus or Buddhists. Often, acceptance of Christianity simply meant a way of reacting against an oppressive social or political order. But, in reality, the European missionaries had little to offer. Their civilization was, in many respects, inferior to the ones they found in China, Japan or India. Their religion was intolerant and cruel, and interfered with cherished beliefs and traditions. The nuclei of Christians scattered everywhere gradually disappeared and only very few would survive until the 19th century. Persecution from local authorities started very quickly and was later reinforced by the Dutch and the English, who were Protestants and exhibited few proselytizing tendencies. In Ethiopia, China and Japan, reaction against the Catholic missionaries brought about bloody persecutions and widespread martyrdom.

Growing intolerance made it more difficult for the Portuguese to maintain good relations with the Asian peoples. The Inquisition was established in India in 1560, and its ominous activities started shortly afterward. Most victims were Hindus and Buddhists, particularly converts to Christianity who were suspected of backsliding.

Of much more interest was the cultural significance of the missions. They contributed to the European knowledge of Asia and to the development of communications between Europe and most of that continent. The Jesuits studied the native languages, customs, beliefs and histories, prepared dictionaries and other means of communication, and exchanged knowledge, methods and ideas. They endeavoured to understand the complex philosophies of India and China as a way of spreading Christianity with fruitful results. They studied philosophy, botany and local zoology, exchanged itineraries and trade possibilities, and established regular communications with the Portuguese trade ports and fortresses.

It was also through the Jesuits that the printing press reached Asia (Goa, Macao and Japan). For the purpose of international contacts, Portuguese became the language of long-distance trade until the 18th century. Portuguese words remained in the local languages and dialects, very many having survived to this day.

A special kind of literature arose, known as travel literature, embracing a great number of itineraries, descriptive letters, reports, diaries and, of course, historical chronicles.

The artistic achievements of the Portuguese in Asia must also be emphasized. It is true that the Portuguese also destroyed some fine examples of native art, but they replaced every monument and endowed India and China with some beautiful examples of Renaissance, Mannerist and Baroque styles.

•

For more than two centuries, the history of Brazil was, above all, the history of a desperate effort to find gold. As a consequence, the boundaries of present-day Brazil had been reached and defined as early as 1638. The connected basins of the Amazon and Paraná-Paraguay rivers permitted a sort of circumnavigation of a huge territory and the establishment of contacts with the Spanish neighbours. The limits of Brazil were defined simply by the existence of settled Spaniards, who never proceeded as far east as the Portuguese did west.

This second «discovery» of Brazil was truly epic, full of unknown heroes and martyrs, and anonymous explorers, though it was also marked by periodic massacres of natives, inevitable hatreds, rivalries and intrigue. However, it also produced magnificent results. Principles of organization were set up for many expeditions, according to the Portuguese late-medieval and 16th-century army constitution which gave the same *bandeira* («flag») to a company of x number of men with an insignia of its own (also called *bandeira)*. Throughout the 17th century, the *bandeiras* went farther and farther in their objectives. In his last and major one (1648-51), Raposo Tavares departed from São Paulo westward, and «circumnavigated» Brazil up to Belém do Pará.

But there were also threats to the expansion of the Portuguese in the definitive constitution of Brazil. The challenge posed by the French and the Dutch, as well as the Spanish counter-expansion, prevented the stretching of Brazilian borders and, for a while, threatened the existence of Brazil itself.

After a first attack on Baía, which the Portuguese and Spaniards were still strong enough to recover, the Dutch centred their efforts on the Pernambuco region. Successively enlarging their area of attack, they gained all the northeast in a few years. Then, they tried to organize their new dominions with a brief period of economic and administrative success.

The economic conjuncture of 1642-44, with a drop in sugar price in Amsterdam, helped to increase discontent against the invaders. In Recife, the Portuguese rose in 1645 and defeated the Dutch. The main effort unquestionably belonged to the settlers, but Lisbon sent its help too. Meanwhile, Angola, the most important source of slaves, had been recaptured by the Portuguese. In 1648-49, the Dutch were twice defeated in the first and second battles of Guararapes. Olinda fell (1648), then Recife (1654), along with all the territory which had been lost to the Dutch.

The rise of Brazil in the late-16th and 17th centuries was reflected in an increase in population: two thousand Portuguese in the 1540s; 25 thousand at the end of the century, excluding civilized natives, black slaves and many other mixed-race inhabitants. Such figures had probably doubled by the middle of the 17th century. The captaincies of Baía and Pernambuco quickly outpaced the others both in population and in economic importance.

A map of the Portuguese colonization of Brazil at that time would have shown only a very narrow fringe of coastal territory effectively conquered. Up until 1650, not even the coastline was thoroughly colonized. Only in the São Paulo and Rio de Janeiro regions did the Portuguese penetration go beyond 100 kilometres.

The absence of white women, the life conditions in which the settlers found the natives and the rise of slavery all led to rampant miscegenation, unparalleled anywhere in the Portuguese empire, except perhaps in Cape Verde. The whites were always considered superior to the others and held most offices of leadership, although tolerance and respect toward both mulattoes and *mamelucos* reached a higher level in Brazil than probably anywhere else.

The Christian missionaries — especially the Jesuits — found in Amerindians ideal subjects for evangelization. The missionaries succeeded very quickly in their purposes and immediately started to organize small Christian Indian groups and to settle them in villages *(aldeias)* and groups of villages *(reduções)* under their direct leadership. Gradually, the Jesuits, with the native masses as a base, created a state of their own within Brazil, which threatened the very authority of the crown.

Black slavery was hardly condemned, even if men like António Vieira tried to protect the blacks from their masters' boundless despotism. The settlers, in turn, quickly realized that Africans made much better slaves than the natives, being stronger, more disciplined and more persistent.

The development of sugar production was the main reason for the importation of slaves. On the whole, the few existing statistics show some 2 thousand to 3 thousand black Africans living in Brazil by 1570, and 13 thousand to 15 thousand by 1600. Slavery and sugar plantations went hand in hand. The culture of sugar cane spread all over Brazil with its main centres at Pernambuco, Baía and, in the mid-1600s, Rio de Janeiro. Sugar allowed the Portuguese crown to give up India without too many economic troubles for the mainland and without too much concern for the future. Other profitable products were brazil-wood, cotton and tobacco, cattle, etc.

All these cultures, which gave strength and prosperity to the colony, favoured the rise of the *latifundium* and the growth of a class of rich landowners and plantation owners. Indeed, the feudal type of economy that the donatory system had introduced in Brazil only developed throughout the 16th and 17th centuries. Their lords *(senhores de engenho)* directly explored only a portion of them, sub-granting the rest to other settlers or farmers *(lavradores)* for a number of years. The *senhor de engenho* was a true feudal lord, with a host of relatives, farmers, artisans, clients and slaves working for him and dependent upon him. Like the ancient feudal cells, the plantation tended and tried to be self-sufficient, reducing imports to a minimum but — a less feudal characteristic — striving for a maximum of exports.

From an administrative point of view, an important change had taken place in the late 1540s: the implementation of a central government for all of Brazil. The 1548 act appointed Tomé de Sousa as the first governor-general. He would build the new capital of Brazil, Baía, and provide for its defence and cultural advancement. He even wanted to create a university, but was unsuccessful.

In a frontier land like Brazil, culture could not have flourished greatly. Schools were scarce, as was the number of intellectuals and available books. No printing press existed. Under Jesuit control, a Royal College of Arts was founded in Baía in the 1570s, the first academic degrees being officially granted in 1575. Incidentally, the official policy of the crown was always to centralize learning and force everyone to study in the mother country. From a cultural standpoint, the only interesting achievements were the study of the native languages and usages, and the consequent publication of grammar and vocabulary books, as well as catechisms.

After John III's policy of abandonment, the Portuguese strongholds in Morocco encompassed only the three fortified towns of Ceuta, Tangiers and Mazagão. The Portuguese restoration of 1640 resulted in the loss of two of the fortresses: Ceuta did not acknowledge the secession and remained faithful to the Spanish monarch, the peace treaty of 1668 confirming its ownership by Spain; Tangiers was given to England by the Portuguese crown as part of Princess Catarina's dowry when she married King Charles II (1661). Only Mazagão remained in Portuguese hands.

Strategically-located on the natural route to the south and the southwest, the island of Madeira developed and prospered as the Portuguese empire grew in extent and economic power. Funchal, capital of Madeira, was indeed a compulsory port of call for most Portuguese navigation throughout the 16th and 17th centuries. This circumstance converted Madeira's economy into a very complex one, because the island depended on exports, imports and re-exports of various kinds. It also made Funchal a busy harbour and gave the town a cosmopolitan aspect.

By the mid-1500s, Madeira's main production was sugar, which was sent all over Europe. But the competition of Brazilian sugar (the price of which was half of that from Madeira) and a disease in the cane gradually decreased production. In the 1630s, Madeira sugar was practically knocked out of the island's economy and taxation. However, Madeira quickly replaced sugar with a new product, which prevented drastic structural changes: wine. The island's wine became as famous and widely exported as sugar had once been, reaching the whole of the Portuguese empire and a good part of Europe. But instead of belonging to predominantly Portuguese firms, the wine trade fell into the hands of foreign traders, mostly English.

In the Azores, the great expansion had ended by the mid-1500s, but the archipelago continued to develop its resources and posed no economic difficulties to the crown. The population of the Azores rose considerably until the late 16th century. Its economy went through very interesting cycles: in the mid-16th century, wheat and wood were clearly in the lead, followed by sugar cane, wine and several other products. By 1670, both wood and sugar cane had practically disappeared from the island's economy; wine, maize, flax (and flaxseed) and oranges competed for second place after wheat.

The Cape Verde archipelago proved a failure as a settlement colony, yet its population increased somewhat or remained constant, in relative prosperity because of the island's location as a necessary port of call for South Atlantic navigation. But the important role played by Cape Verde, which accounted for its survival, also brought about a number of catastrophes. The French, the English and the Dutch called on the archipelago as well, stealing both cattle and inhabitants.

Several trade ports depended upon the Santiago government which the Portuguese successfully set up along the African coast, from Arguin (in present-day Mauritania) to Sierra Leone. Those places depended on the gold, chilli, ivory and slave trade, and they never ceased to prosper and grow more numerous throughout the 17th century.

In the Gulf of Guinea, the Portuguese had some 12 to 15 trade ports by the early 17th century. The whole territory under Portuguese control formed the captaincy of Mina, with headquarters in São Jorge da Mina (Elmina) and the São Tomé captaincy, with its headquarters in the island and city of São Tomé. For religious purposes, the whole area depended on the bishop of São Tomé. Indeed, this isle was the true economic and political centre of Portuguese power north of Angola. Both captaincies were crown colonies, although the islands of Príncipe and Ano Bom belonged to hereditary captains subject to the authority of the captain-general and governor of São Tomé. Mina had lived on gold and spice trade, while São Tomé depended on sugar exports. In the 1570s, São Tomé was a great producer and exporter of very cheap sugar. There were more than 20 sugar mills and the slave imports increased.

In a few years, all this had changed. A disease in the sugar cane, slave rebellions, attacks by French and Dutch pirates, and Brazilian competition ruined the economy of São Tomé. From a prosperous plantation colony, São Tomé became a mere slave entrepot where slaves were easier to obtain than in Angola. It was more because of this and strategic reasons than due to their economic value that the Dutch endeavoured to conquer the Portuguese possessions in the Gulf of Guinea. One by one, all the trade ports on the mainland fell in the 1620s and 1630s: São Jorge da Mina surrendered in 1637. The final storming of São Tomé took place in 1641. Yet, inland, the Dutch could not get through. Príncipe and Ano Bom never fell. In 1648, Salvador Correia de Sá was able to reconquer the city after liberating Angola.

The unsuccessful experiment of a protectorate in the Congo led the Portuguese to try another way in Angola. Thus, in 1574, Angola was made into a captaincy (*capitania* or *donataria*), and granted to Paulo Dias de Novais, following some of the rules of the captaincy system in the Atlantic islands and Brazil. He founded Luanda as the capital (1576), and built some fortresses as decided in the contract. But when he died (1589), the Portuguese were far from being firmly settled in Angola, although they ruled over part of the coastline. The black indigenous people, who were much more civilized and better organized than the Americans, offered strong and permanent resistance. The climate killed hundreds of settlers and weakened many others. The soil was far less fertile than in Brazil. And the slave trade diverted almost everyone from agriculture. Also, it made Angola a «colony», first of São Tomé and, later, Brazil, where slave labour was essential to the plantations.

The crown put an end to the captaincy system and replaced it with a general-government (1590). Governor Manuel Cerveira Pereira founded Benguela (1617) and assumed control of a vast track of coastline. In 1641, the Dutch managed to capture Luanda and thus control the main source of slaves to Brazil. The Portuguese retreated inland, and for seven years a series of acts of warfare followed by temporary truce marked the history of Angola. With the Portuguese close to complete surrender, the Brazilian settlers sent a relief expedition under the command of Salvador Correia de Sá, who succeeded in recapturing Luanda and expelling the Dutch from all of Angola (1648). In a few years, governor Correia de Sá (1648-52) and his successors imposed the crown's control, if not effective rule, over great part of the hinterland.

ABSOLUTISM AND ENLIGHTENED DESPOTISM

The year 1667 marked the beginning of a long period of political stability in Portugal, which would end only with the French invasions. To begin with, three long reigns ensured continuity: those of Pedro II (1667 to 1706), as regent and king, John V (1706 to 1750) and José I (1750 to 1777). Maria's relatively brief period of rule (1777 to 1792) was followed by another long one, that of her son John VI as regent and as king (1792 to 1826). Royal continuity was matched by secretarial continuity. Governmental stability had its advantages but also its inconveniences: if it permitted reforms, it also favoured conservatism and routine. Which of the two prevailed very much depended upon the sovereign's character, the secretary's personality and, above all, the circumstances of the epoch.

The succession to the Spanish throne was Portugal's excuse for a change in external policy, as a way to obtain more advantageous boundaries in the metropolis as well in Brazil. Fifty years of peace followed, interrupted only by a brief intervention by John V in the Mediterranean to help the Pope and Venice fight the Turks.

When John died (1750), his son José I entrusted full power to a former diplomat, Sebastião José de Carvalho e Melo, a representative of the lower aristocracy who the monarch successively promoted to Count of Oeiras (1759) and to Marquis of Pombal (1770). Pombal controlled not only government but also the whole country by levelling down all possible opposition, and even the king himself, who had little talent for ruling. The earthquake that occurred on November 1, 1755, destroying half of Lisbon and a good part of southern Portugal, enhanced Pombal's prestige because of the strict measures which were immediately adopted in the emergency to restore order, tend to the dead and wounded, and rebuild the city.

After eight years of outraging the nobility and humiliating it in various ways, Pombal's government aroused a wide conspiracy of aristocrats with the aim of getting rid of José and enthroning his heiress, Maria. Led by the Duke of Aveiro, there was an attempt to kill the monarch, but it failed (1758). A mock trial led to death at the stake of one duke, two marquises and one marchioness, one count and several servants and clients. Other nobles were punished or banished. The Jesuits, accused of taking part in the plot, were expelled from the country.

Portugal tried to remain neutral in the Seven Years War (1756-63), without success: Spanish and French troops invaded the province of Trás-os-Montes (1762). The signing of the Paris Peace Treaty (1763) prevented any possible disasters.

From 1777 to 1786, Maria I ruled together with her husband Pedro III. Late in 1791, she became insane and, when all hopes of recovery were given up, her son John took over the regency (1792).

In external policy, instead of Pombal's firm attitudes and clear alliance with England, Maria I and John fostered a dubious diplomacy of compromise with England, France and Spain. The French Revolution and the war between France and most of Europe made Portugal's external policy extremely difficult to manage. Secret negotiations and agreements between France and Spain presaged an invasion and conquest of Portugal. War was declared (1801) with disastrous consequences. A hasty peace treaty forced the Portuguese to surrender the town of Olivença to Spain and to pay a heavy indemnity.

Late in 1806, Napoleon decreed the continental blockade. In August 1807, the French and Spanish diplomatic envoys in Lisbon delivered an ultimatum to the Portuguese government: either it declared war on England, or the French and Spanish armies would invade the country. The treaty signed at Fontainebleau between France and Spain divided Portugal into three parts: the province of Entre-Douro-e-Minho as the «Kingdom of Northern Lusitania»; Alentejo and the Algarve as the principality of the Algarves; while the rest of Portugal would be disposed of when general peace came. In mid-November, the French general Junot crossed the Portuguese border with a large army and started the invasion. The Portuguese government did not think of opposing the French and gave orders to stop all resistance and welcome the invaders in Lisbon. The royal family, the government and hundreds of people embarked for Brazil late in November (when Junot was almost at the city gates) arriving in South America early in 1808. The new capital of the kingdom was established in Rio and for 14 years Portugal was nothing more than a colony of Brazil.

Junot ruled the country as a conquered land under military occupation. The Portuguese army was disbanded and converted into a «Portuguese Legion», sent to France and elsewhere to fight under Napoleon. Popular resistance started immediately, and a guerrilla war started against the invaders. In June 1808, Prince-regent John was acclaimed in the north, a *Provisional Junta* being established under the supreme command of the bishop of Porto. The revolution spread everywhere, stimulated by a retreat of the Spanish troops and by news of rebellions against the French in Spain. Supported by this wide popular movement, the English, under the future Lord Wellington, landed in Galicia (northern Spain), entered Portugal and forced Junot to ask for truce. In September, the French embarked headed for home, taking with them most of their loot.

Relative order could be restored everywhere, and defence against a new French attack was immediately organized under the command of English general William Beresford, to whom full powers were given. He practically ruled the country until 1820.

The second French invasion began in February 1809, under the command of marshall Soult. The French entered Portugal through Trás-os-Montes and conquered the whole of the north, to the Douro River. Yet his forces could not stand the Anglo-Portuguese pressure and retreated to Spain in May 1809.

In the Autumn of that same year, and foreseeing a new French attack, Lord Wellington organized a proper defence for Lisbon. Three fortified lines *(linhas de Torres Vedras)* surrounding the capital to about twenty miles were built, and the city became impregnable. Indeed, when marshal Masséna, leading a strong army, invaded Portugal (July 1810), he stopped at the lines, after a first defeat at Buçaco. Early in March 1811, the French began to retreat. Besides restoring Portugal's independence and integrity, the Vienna Congress (1814-15) gave the town of Olivença back to Portugal, but the Spaniards never complied.

Four years of war had left the country in poor condition. The French invasions and occupation had devastated a large part of Portugal. The country was both an English protectorate and a Brazilian colony. The government was located in Rio; in Portugal, there was only a regency. British officers served in the Portuguese army, which was becoming entirely English in organization. King John VI (Maria I had died in 1816) had no wish to return to Europe. The regency kept intact the old methods of government, showing no disposition whatsoever to adjust to modern ideas. A ferocious persecution of all liberals took place. Throughout the country, discontent against the king, the English and the regency were accompanied by a deplorable economic and financial situation. Revolutionary ferment was everywhere and would soon lead to open rebellion.

•

By the middle of the 17th century, Portugal was home to some two million people. This basic figure remained fairly constant until 1732. But from then on, the rise was continuous, reaching around 3 100 000 by 1820. Lisbon's population in the 1600s, in itself too large for the size of Portugal, stagnated or increased only slightly: by 1780, there were 150 thousand people, some 180 thousand at the end of the century, and 200 thousand in 1820. Instead of being an international competitor for the title of «great city», as before, Lisbon declined to the level of second-class city, just as Portugal's position declined relative to other nations. On the other hand, Porto went from housing more than 20 thousand in 1732, to 50 thousand inhabitants by 1820. It was a good example of northern prosperity and economic development, in contrast to the decline of most of the south.

In the economic sphere, the complex structure of this time had a common denominator: trade with Brazil. This trade produced most of the crown revenue; it determined the coming of foreign vessels to Lisbon and other Portuguese ports as well as a flourishing network of foreign connections; money was plentiful and stable; it permitted the maintenance of surpluses in the commercial balance; and it allowed bountiful investments.

However, Brazil's importance should not make us forget the reality and the growth of a Portuguese European economy, based on agriculture and trade, and even the beginnings of a local industry.

The economic doctrines of mercantilism favoured the development of national crafts for export as a way of obtaining gold and balancing external trade. After some attempts of little significance, it was only under the government of Pombal that a more fruitful policy was carried out. For eight years, the government helped to set up hundreds of small factories. Only the cotton and silk manufactures, however, survived and prospered.

Portuguese commerce with foreign countries depended mostly on her colonies. Sugar, tobacco, cotton, slaves, spices and diamonds were the principal sources of revenue. Three quarters of the country's imports from abroad went to Brazil, India and Africa.

Yet Portugal alone had much to sell and to purchase: wine, olive oil, salt, leather and fruit. The chief product of the 18th century was undoubtedly wine, mostly Port wine, which brought prosperity to a part of the country but also bound Portugal to England, her largest wine buyer. The wine was largely in the hands of English merchants and firms. From Europe, Portugal continued to purchase an immense variety of manufactured goods. Textiles always held first place. In 1703, the Treaty of Methuen was signed between Portugal and England, according to which English woollen cloths and other woollen manufactures would enter Portugal unrestrictedly, while all Portuguese wines would enter England, under the same taxation as the French ones. Commercial and industrial developments greatly depended upon a conscious economic policy of setting up chartered companies and monopolies, namely in Pombal's period.

The discovery of gold mines in Brazil could solve the problem of the balance of trade deficit. In 1699, Lisbon received the first 514 kilograms of gold. Gold output increased over the following years until 1720. With so much gold for nearly a century, and with a prosperous balance of trade afterward, it is not surprising that currency remained strong and underwent very few changes in value. Most of the gold was sent to England, Holland, Genoa and other areas. It stimulated the whole European economy, particularly England's. But the Peninsular War put an end to prosperity. Revenues declined as both external and internal trade were paralyzed for long periods. The Portuguese monopoly of Brazil ended.

A symptom of the concentration of power in the hands of a few was the decline of government by councils. Under John V, government belonged more and more to the cabinet, while the councils' powers faded away. In 1736, a government reform vested more power in the secretaries of State, whose number and specialization increased. Important reforms also took place in the areas of justice and finance. A law in 1790 theoretically abolished seigniorial justice, ending the feudal rights concerning jurisdiction and the entrance of royal officials.

The rise in taxation and Brazilian gold gave the king the means to control the nobles by way of allowances and gifts. The old nobility was forced to accept the rising competition of bureaucrats, men of letters and, later, rich traders. The complexity of the state's functions enhanced the role of the bureaucrats and required special preparation for the administrative offices (including diplomacy), which the nobles no longer had. The economy also needed specialists. Trade was officially declared a noble, necessary, and profitable profession. The renewal of the aristocracy over than a century was almost complete. Title granting became a simple reward, given to anyone, regardless of lineage.

For the clergy, the period was one of continuous and steep decline. The spirit of the 18th century was one of doubt, impiety, and even atheism. The clergy itself became closer to the lay world and abandoned much of its religious discipline and beliefs. With the strengthening of the royal power and centralization, ecclesiastical privileges and prerogatives were constantly curbed. No new orders were created. The religious population of the monasteries declined. But, at the same time, the number of nonreligious dependents in the monasteries increased.

In the meantime, the Jesuits had been expelled from the kingdom (1759) and their society dissolved by Pope Clement XIV. They had shown to be unable to keep up with the development of education and science, and their intellectual prestige no longer ranked as high as it had been. Their existence as a state within the state was incompatible with the despotic monarchies of the 18th century.

Something similar happened to the Inquisition, wich had become another state within the state. Throughout the late-17th and the first half of the 18th centuries, it continued to persecute «Jews», «heretics» and others, i.e. middle-class people including a high percentage of businessmen, traders and artisans. Like the Jesuits, the Inquisition had been left behind by the times and was incapable of understanding and adjusting to the changes. In 1769, Pombal felt strong enough to destroy it as an independent tribunal and converted the Inquisition into a royal court entirely dependent upon the government. The distinction between Old Christians and New Christians was abolished, and all discrimination based on blood ceased. Public *autos da fé* disappeared along with the death penalty.

The secular clergy prospered, as long as it remained subservient to the king's wishes. Important privileges and allowances enhanced the wealth and the pomp of the Church, particularly around the king. Five new bishoprics were created between 1770 and 1774. Yet, all this pomp and affluence brought about worldliness and lack of independence. Much like the aristocracy, the clergy became dependent on the royal favour. Cardinals, archbishops, bishops, canons, deans and others formed a numerous Church aristocracy little different from the upper nobility.

Foreign traders settled in Lisbon and in Porto controlled most, or at least the most profitable part, of the trade with Europe. They too helped prevent the development of a Portuguese upper-bourgeoisie, as well as the establishment of «modern» credit institutions like banks. Nearly all over Portugal there was, nonetheless, a petty bourgeoisie of traders and artisans. They controlled practically all the internal currents of traffic, as well as maritime trade. By the late-1700s, the rise in trade itself had promoted the Portuguese bourgeoisie to a significant role. A small group of rich traders joined the aristocracy by being given noble titles.

Among the lower classes, the role played by artisans should be emphasized too, with their numbers very much increased. Many foreign artisans also came to Portugal and stayed there permanently, thus strengthening the workers' ranks.

As a social group, the armed forces started to rise throughout the 18th century, when they were organized as a permanent body. Commanding roles now required some special qualifications and a proper curriculum. In short, being an officer became a profession. Officers planned fortifications and public buildings, supervised the setting up of new industries, or studied how to bring water to a city. Most officers still belonged to the aristocracy, but some came from humbler origins, namely the bourgeoisie and the bureaucracy. Army and navy officers began to have a social consciousness of their own and a sense of closeness to other «modern» groups such as bureaucrats and traders. Together with the former, they represented the elite of the new rising bourgeois class.

•

The new and expanding economic power, the rising complexity of administration and the development of international contacts required new methods of government and interference in every area of life. Royal absolutism was thus carried to its final consequences, i.e. the doctrine that the king's authority was boundless and that the limits of the state's power were the state itself. Based on reason, despotism claimed that usages and customs played no part at all; it avowed that the laws of nature were interpreted by the king, that the laws of God were deposited upon the king himself, with the Church's submission to his will and, finally, that the laws of the realm did not apply to the monarch. In this way, *enlightened despotism* tended to subjugate all social classes to the royal power, to abolish any privileges based upon heredity and tradition, to reject any political and social organs of control over the central administration, and to foster the rise of a national Church independent of Rome. It favoured industrialism and new techniques for combatting imports from abroad; it supported monopolies and economic protectionism; it developed bureaucracy. In the cultural arena, it had to adopt secularization by means of direct intervention in the public education (and cultural) system, and a strong state censorship.

Enlightened despotism started in Portugal under José's reign, particularly after 1755, and became the general governing doctrine until 1820. Its chief architect was the Marquis of Pombal who, in part, adopted theoretical principles espoused by some

Portuguese philosophers and pedagogues who had lived abroad, or by some of his predecessors in government and diplomacy.

Besides the law, the other vast field where Enlightenment played a decisive role was culture. The backwardness of the Portuguese education system was stressed by all those who compared it to advanced European countries. The Portuguese who lived abroad or who travelled extensively in Europe *(estrangeirados)* were instrumental in defining the many faults and preparing the total revision of the Portuguese system.

The cultural revolution also meant the replacement of Spanish influence by French, English, Italian and German ones. The cultural unity of the Iberian Peninsula was thus severed and, with it, the possibility of a political union. The Portuguese began to look at Spain as an obstacle to contact with France and the rest of Europe. Gradually, Portugal became less Iberian and more European. Spanish, which had been Portugal's second language, gave way to French. In the arts, the Baroque, considered a Spanish corruption of the pure classical models, was forsaken for French and Italian classicism.

One of the main arenas where the new «lights» could be discussed was the academies. The most important of all Portuguese academies was the Royal Academy of Science, founded in 1779. One of its purposes was to connect the university with the development of economic and scientific research. It organized a scientific museum and an excellent library with foreign and Portuguese books; it participated in or fostered numerous projects of reform; and had contacts with academies and institutions in Europe and America.

Journalism and the writing of memoirs provided another kind of literary expression. After some premature attempts in the mid-1600s, the first newspaper with some continuity was *Gazeta de Lisboa,* which started publication in 1715. Other newspapers appeared throughout the century and in the early-1800s, some devoted to general news, others to literary or economic subjects. State censorship, however, particularly severe after 1750, prevented the development of a free press as it existed in England or in Holland.

The scientific movement was certainly more modest but no less important. Many books appeared on science and technology, along with translations and adaptations into Portuguese of foreign treaties and handbooks. Father Bartolomeu de Gusmão invented a flying machine which went up to the ceiling in the ballroom of the royal palace and then again in the open air (1709). New techniques and technological devices were introduced, with practical purposes. Machines of all kinds were imported. The setting was thus prepared for the great educational reforms which tried to adjust official education in Portugal to the general progress in every field of knowledge, particularly science.

The religious order of St. Philip Nery (Oratorians) had been among the first to fight Jesuit control of education and to denounce its backwardness. Pombal's radical reforms covered the primary, secondary and university levels. In 1759, the University of Évora was shut down, along with the expulsion of its owners, the Jesuits. The University of Coimbra's new statutes were issued in 1772. Besides the existing schools of Theology, Canons, Law and Medicine, Pombal created the colleges of Mathematics and natural Philosophy (i.e. Sciences), providing them with an astronomical observatory, a museum of natural history, laboratories of physics and chemistry, a laboratory of medicine, a pharmacy and a botanical garden. Schools for nautical studies and design were opened, as well as military and commercial classes. A Royal Printing Press was set up in 1768. Pombal's cultural reforms did not die with his downfall; on the contrary, they were maintained and enlarged, namely with a Royal Academy of the Navy and a Military School. At the same time, the enlightened principle of spreading culture was furthered when the king's library opened its doors to the public as the first Royal Public Library in Portugal (1796).

It must be emphasized that all these important cultural changes did not imply cultural freedom. Censorship ceased to be primarily religious and generally backward in spirit, but it continued on political grounds. However, there is no doubt that a greater freedom gradually arose from the new cosmopolitan spirit of «reason» and «enlightenment». Every intellectual, nobleman and bureaucrat owned, read and disseminated forbidden books. Many approved works, even if seemingly harmless, actually undermined the bases of the old regime, the inviolability of religious beliefs and doctrines of despotism, if not of royalty itself.

Until the mid-18th century, the baroque style entirely permeated Portugal, helped by the prosperity of the period. But, at the same time, Italian and German masters were invited into the country and started building in a less adorned and more classical way. The German architect Ludwig built the huge monastery of Mafra, and many other sober and elegant buildings. Italian architect Nazoni was active in the north of Portugal (church and tower of the Clérigos, in Porto), among others. Of the more useful and practical buildings, a special reference should be made to the long and artistic aqueduct which solved the problem of water supply to Lisbon *(Aqueduto das Águas Livres)*.

The great event that influenced the arts, however, was the earthquake which destroyed about half of Lisbon in November 1, 1755. Instead of having the city rebuilt according to the old plan, Pombal had the rebuilding follow new conceptions in urbanism and architecture. He chose a very simple yet revolutionary plan that transformed most of Lisbon into a huge chessboard, starting at a vast square opening out to the river. In that square, the government offices were built, as well as a triumphal arch and an elegant statue of King José on horseback. Accordingly, Lisbon became a truly «enlightened» city, rationally-planned and built, its streets, squares and houses drawn with a ruler in the most theoretical way an 18th-century philosopher could envision.

Besides Lisbon, with its new palaces, churches and fountains, a beautiful royal country house was built in Queluz (near Lisbon), modelled after the French palace of Versailles; a sumptuous palace was built in Ajuda; and many other noble or bourgeois residences displayed, throughout the country, the «restoration of the arts» defended by the classicists.

BRAZIL

The creation of the general-government in Brazil in the mid-16th century had very much reduced the autonomy of each captaincy and the consequent powers of each captain. But the colony was too large to be governed like the mainland; and the growing needs of territorial expansion brought about a political, social and economic structure altogether opposed to centralization. The general-government retained its powers of ensuring defence, but gradually lost many others related to administration, economy and finance. The development of the interior brought about the establishment of new units, such as Minas Gerais, Goiás, Mato Grosso, São José do Rio Negro, etc.

In 1763, the headquarters of the general-government was moved from Baía to Rio de Janeiro, as the economic and political centre of Brazil was also moving southward. In 1772, with the extinction of the state of Maranhão, the two Brazils became forever united and the administrative changes undertaken throughout a whole century were accomplished. The ecclesiastical division changed even more, showing the tremendous development of the colony throughout the 17th and 18th centuries. Thus, in the late-1700s, Catholic Brazil encompassed one archbishopric, that of Baía, and ten other dioceses.

The rise of Brazil was also apparent through the increase in her population. With some 50 thousand whites and just under 100 thousand others (excluding the native Indians), by the middle of the 17th century, Brazil proudly registered more than 1 500 000 people in the 1770s, growing more than tenfold, the highest rate of increase in America. Of all these people, a little more than half were probably black slaves. Baía and Rio de Janeiro were home to more than 50 thousand inhabitants in 1780, having become the second and third cities in the Portuguese empire, immediately after Lisbon. Most of this growth resulted, of course, from immigration. The gold rush and further news of Brazil's affluence appealed to thousands in Portugal, coming from all over the country but particularly from the north and from the islands of Madeira and the Azores.

Another proof of Brazil's expansion was found in the conquest of the new lands in the interior. By comparing maps of the colony in 1650 and in 1750, one can see the immense addition of newly-settled or explored territory. Overall, about a half of present-day Brazil was explored and her native population subjected to Portuguese rule. This fact was internationally acknowledged when the Treaty of Madrid (1750) between Spain and Portugal formally replaced the old and forgotten Tordesillas demarcation of 1494 with a new border roughly identical to that of present-day Brazil.

Late in the 17th century, gold, which had been sought for so long, was finally found. Ore beds with gold, emeralds and other precious stones were successively discovered until the 1720s. The most important gold mines were located in what is now Minas Gerais («General Mines»), a name that clearly suggests the importance of that area. Gold became the cornerstone of Brazilian economy. Its peak of expansion roughly coincided with the reign of John V, quickly declining in Pombal's time.

The general consensus was that sugar was next in Brazil's productions. However, sugar ranked in value above gold and diamonds combined for many, many years. Throughout the first half to the 18th century, more and more sugar was being shipped to Europe: Italy and other Mediterranean countries absorbed most of it, while Portugal and her empire were by no means unimportant buyers. But the decline began due to West Indies competition. Using more efficient techniques, which led to a remarkable increase in yield, sugar from Central America ousted Brazilian sugar from the European markets.

Both mining and sugar plantations required cheap and abundant labour. Later on, cotton, tobacco and other extensive plantations needed this labour too. It is not surprising, then, that slave imports from Africa jumped to unprecedented figures. A tentative number of two million for the period 1700-1820 would probably be a fair estimate.

As well as the three mainstays of Brazilian economy in the 18th century — gold and diamonds, sugar, and slaves — there were many other lesser but not insignificant commercial items: tobacco, cotton, rice, fibres, dyestuffs, cacao, hides, etc. Horses, too, were bred in large quantities.

The growth of a landed aristocracy in Brazil had started much before the end of the 17th century, an obvious consequence of the quasi-feudal structure introduced by Portuguese settlers and government. The growth of the *latifundium* brought about the rise of an upper class of large landowners, mostly white yet frequently mixed with black or Indian blood. They soon had to compete with a flourishing bourgeoisie of traders in the main ports, doubled by the growing bureaucracy (jurists, lawyers, clerks), army officers and several other professions. Despite some conflicts, expressed through several local riots and competition in town administration, landed proprietors, traders and civil servants managed to get along together within the general framework of being Brazilians. Instead, there was rising opposition to the mother country and to the Portuguese appointed to offices in Brazil.

The religious orders played a very relevant role in exploring and colonizing Brazil. Among the many orders which exerted influence, the Jesuits undoubtedly took the lead. They had built a true kingdom by the middle of the 18th century, from Amazonia to the River Plate, although their main fiefs lay in the Paraná-Uruguay basins. They were the lords of hundreds of thousands of black slaves and had under their direction armies of thousands of Amerindians. In the *reduções* (groups of villages) and *aldeias* (villages), their power tolerated interference from neither settlers nor crown representatives. From a political standpoint, the Jesuits soon threatened both the policy of centralization carried out by the crown and the very definition of Brazil's boundaries.

Pombal, who was then full master in Lisbon, could not tolerate such a defiance of his government's orders. When he found he could accuse the Jesuits of plotting to kill the king, he expelled them from Portugal and all her overseas dominions (1759). Two years afterward, he declared all Brazilian Indians to be free and strictly forbade any act of enslavement by the settlers. Cheered by most people, the arrest and expulsion of the Jesuits could be carried out with much less trouble than one might believe. The rural properties of the order passed into the hands of the crown, and were immediately auctioned off.

The secular clergy, more interested in administrative problems and in providing bureaucratic or teaching personnel to the civilized areas, neglected the missions and became thoroughly integrated into white society. In Brazil, as elsewhere, the late-1700s and early-1800s brought about the decline of the secular clergy, the religious orders, and of the Church in general.

•

It was in the north that Brazil's borders were first established, after long negotiations with France. The Treaty of Utrecht (1713) defined the final border of Brazil at the Oiapoque River, where it is still located today. From 1809 to 1815, the Portuguese occupied French Guiana in response to Napoleon's invasion of Portugal.

The Portuguese had always claimed the River Plate as their southern border, but had done little or nothing to enforce that claim. In 1680, they decided to try a definitive occupation of «their» territory, founding a settlement at Sacramento on the northern branch of the River Plate. The founding of Sacramento was an attempt — an unsuccessful one — to control the silver stream from the Potosi mines in what is now Bolivia. Actually, what the Portuguese got from it derived from cattle rearing alone. The Spaniards immediately realized the danger of a Portuguese fixation; as a result, the history of the Sacramento colony consisted mostly of political and/or military strife, with alternate victories for either party. The Treaty of San Ildefonso (1777) definitely put Sacramento in Spanish hands. Later attempts from Portugal to absorb Uruguay showed that the problem had not been satisfactorily resolved.

The definition of the western border owed much to the Jesuit and Carmelite missions established all over the Amazon basin, but no less to the daring expeditions of 17th- and 18th-century *bandeirantes*. By the mid-1700s, a series of advance posts had been established, justifying the claims of Portuguese diplomacy.

Brazil's general prosperity, along with the wise administrative policy followed by the crown throughout the 18th century, smoothed over rebellions or autonomous tendencies for a long time. But it was obvious that the American revolution and the rise of new political ideologies would have their impact on the colony sooner or later. Minas Gerais, the most troubled and active of all Brazilian captaincies, led the way. A small *intelligentzia* had risen there, quite receptive to modern currents of thought. Second-lieutenant *(alferes)* Joaquim José da Silva Xavier, known as *Tiradentes* (literally, «tooth-puller»), led a conspiracy against Portugal, vaguely aiming at the secession of Minas under a republican government and at the abolition of slavery. The plot (the so-called *Inconfidência Mineira*) was discovered (1789), its members arrested, and *Tiradentes* was executed. In 1798, another republican plot, this time in Baía, gathered together some low-class coloureds and slaves. The execution of four of the leaders easily suppressed it.

Brazil had reached political maturity and the question of her independence would only be a matter of years. Demographically, the colony's growth was parallel to that of the motherland: more than 1 500 000 people in the 1770s, 2 500 000 by the end of the century, 3 600 000 in 1819. About half of Brazil's population were black (mostly slaves), more than one-fourth were mixed-race, and the remaining were «whites». It is to the latter that the independence movement must be credited. They resented the maintenance of a colonial status, which prevented them from trading directly with foreign countries; they complained of Lisbon's great distance for solving administrative and political matters; they accused the officials sent from Lisbon of corruption, despotism, etc.

Yet Brazil's progress toward autonomy did not follow the same pattern as the other American countries. In November 1807, when Napoleon's army invaded and occupied Portugal, King John VI and most of his government and court decided to take refuge in Brazil. Thus, Brazil became the motherland and Portugal the colony. This situation lasted for 13 years. A new nation was gradually rising from the American colony, and John's rule there was concerned with setting up the much-needed political, administrative, economic and cultural framework for Brazil's full emergence.

An act of 1808, confirmed and defined by the treaty of 1810, marked the true end of colonial status. Ships no longer had to proceed to Portugal and pay duties there before their cargoes could be forwarded anywhere in the world. As England was then Portugal's foremost buyer and seller, the act of 1808 benefited her immensely, while dealing a cruel blow to Portugal's trade.

In 1815, the inevitable political-administrative step was taken: Brazil became a kingdom, with her own royal institutions. Following the British pattern, a United Kingdom of Portugal, Brazil, and Algarve was created, with equal rights and duties for each part.

Events in Portugal determined the final independence of Brazil. A revolution broke out in August 1820, and one of the first acts of the new constitutional government was to demand the return of the king. After much hesitation, John VI went back, along with the whole court, disembarking in Lisbon amidst general contentment in July 1821. His son Pedro stayed in Rio as regent of the kingdom, heading a separate cabinet.

Yet the return of the monarch to Lisbon could not be well accepted. Brazil was now used to having a king and a court of her own, with the full seat of administration established in her own territory. This understandable feeling was further intensified by the awkward attitude of the first Portuguese constitutional parliament, controlled by the Portuguese bourgeoisie, which adopted a policy intending to force Brazil to give up her new privileges and go back to the old colonial status.

This Brazil could not endure. After having decided to stay, defying the resolution taken by the *cortes,* Pedro was proclaimed

«Perpetual defender of Brazil» in May 1822, and later proclaimed the country's independence (September 1822).

•

Among the remnants of a glorious past, Mazagão was certainly the most useless of all Portuguese dominions. After an uneventful history, Pombal's government rightly appraised the situation and ordered Mazagão to be abandoned when a powerful Muslim army besieged the fortress in 1769.

Madeira and Azores had very few colonial features, even in those days. Populated by an almost all-white population, very like the motherland in most institutions, social patterns, and economic circumstances, they were rapidly tending toward the status of distant appendages of Portugal. Madeira depended on maritime traffic and on the export of wine, both of which expanded, with fluctuations, during the late-17th and the 18th centuries. In the Azores, the decline of wood and wheat was rapidly matched by the export of oranges, flax and maize. Funchal, Angra and Ponta Delgada became large provincial towns, displaying relative affluence in their baroque palaces and lavishly-decorated churches.

The histories of Cape Verde and Guinea were tied together. The islands and the coastline depended on each other, particularly in the slave trade. Pombal's reforms had reached Cape Verde too: a short-lived captaincy-general was made to encompass all the islands and Guinea as well. Cape Verde, like most Portuguese possessions, experienced the dangers of many international wars. In 1712, the French attacked and plundered both Ribeira Grande and Praia. In 1798, they came again and sacked Brava. The English also tried to gain a footing on several of the islands by both peaceful and military means. In Guinea, they founded a trade port in Bolama in the last years of the 18th century.

São Tomé appeared in those days as one of the most corrupt colonies in the Portuguese empire. Power was held by the local «aristocracy» of slave traders and landed mulattoes, who controlled the municipal council *(câmara)* and spent their time quarrelling with the island's other force, the clergy. The crown-appointed captains could do little or nothing to enforce order and royal decisions.

Pombal's government managed to change this state of affairs slightly. Príncipe had been bought by the crown from its hereditary captain (1753). Pombal elevated its main village, Santo António, to a town, and made it the capital of the colony. A new captain-general was appointed, with authority over the one in São Tomé. This legislation did not heal the wound but lessened its effects. By the end of the 18th century, the situation had improved, despite some French attacks on Príncipe. Meanwhile, Portugal had realized the uselessness of some of her possessions in the Gulf of Guinea. Most of the trade ports on the mainland were abandoned and Fernando Pó, along with Ano Bom, were ceded to Spain.

Angola's role as Brazil's most important supplier of slaves continued throughout the 17th and 18th centuries. As the Portuguese territories in South America grew, Angola's position as a labour supplier did too. In the late-1600s, a series of military campaigns gave the Portuguese a still firmer hold on Angola, both on the coastline and inland. During the 18th century, several expeditions departed from Luanda and Benguela for trade, military or purely geographical purposes.

When Pombal took over government, he found Angola's trade in a state of general expansion which dated from the 1720s and which probably led him and his advisers to the erroneous assumption that the colony could be converted into another Brazil. Pombal's great act — which affected not only Angola but most of Portugal's dominions — was to declare freedom of trade for the Portuguese, abolishing the crown monopoly. Governor Francisco de Sousa Coutinho (1764-72) tried hard to stimulate agriculture, trade (other than slavery), settlement, and even industry. But Pombal's and Sousa Coutinho's efforts in Angola generally failed. Until 1790, a new wave of stagnation and decline affected the colony, except for the slave trade with Brazil.

In the early-19th century, the first attempt to connect Angola and Mozambique by land was successful, when the mulatto traders *(pombeiros)* Pedro João Baptista and Amaro José left Cassanje and reached Tete, and returned home the same way (1806-15).

The role of the Portuguese East African dominions throughout this period was still more insignificant. Mozambique continued to depend upon India, both economically and administratively. It was further disrupted by foreign attacks and wars with the natives. In 1688, the Arabs from Oman besieged Mombasa, and with it Pate and Zanzibar. Later, in the 1720s and 1730s, the Dutch and the British often tried to settle down in Lourenço Marques. In the 1740s, French piracy in Mozambique waters began.

Mozambique was given a new lease of life under Pombal's government. The colony was promoted to a separate captaincy (1752). Lourenço Marques was recaptured, while Tete, Inhambane and Mossuril were fortified. In the late-18th and early-19th centuries, Mozambique enjoyed a slight expansion. In order to explore the interior and reach Angola by land, an expedition under Lacerda e Almeida left Tete (1798) but went no further than Cazende.

By the late-1600s, Portuguese power in India was reduced to Diu, Damão, Bassein and a few other fortified towns in the north, and to Goa, with its dependencies, in the south. Despite its continuous decline and loss of population, Goa, the capital, continued to be too huge a head for such a small body. It was still configured as Lisbon or Rome in the East, with a great number of administrative, economic and religious institutions that no longer made any sense.

After a long period of threats, humiliations and open conflicts, the Marathas took possession of Bassein and of all the other northern dependencies, with the exception of Diu and Damão (1739). Shortly afterward, they attacked Goa. Chaul had to be abandoned to them. Yet Portugal recovered with a long series of campaigns which lasted into the 1750s, and then again from 1779 to 1795. Final victory was theirs. A territory four times larger than their possessions in the south, although half as populous, was attached to Goa, and became known as *Novas Conquistas* (New Conquests).

Pombal regarded Portuguese India realistically. The pompous title of viceroy was dropped and replaced by that of governor. He decreed that the Christian natives, regardless of their race and colour, should be considered equal to the Portuguese from Portugal for all public offices and even for landownership. An act of 1774 also abolished the Inquisition in Goa.

Pombal's policy stimulated a counteraction, in some respects more severe in Goa than elsewhere. The Inquisition reappeared (1779), albeit in a very moderate way. The title of viceroy was again given to the governors of India. From 1801 to 1813, Goa — like Portugal after 1807 — was practically under British occupation, with all her forts manned by English garrisons. It was then that the useless Inquisition was once more and forever abolished (1812).

In China, the Portuguese kept Macao, not as a crown colony — as they often liked to pretend — but simply as a favour from the Chinese to whom they were useful as traders. Until the 19th century, Macao was more like a feudal territory in the Iberian manner than a European colony. Power belonged to the local municipal council or senate, which gave Macao the curious aspect of a tiny urban republic. Economically speaking, Macao brought good profits to the crown, despite her gradual decline throughout the 18th century.

The easternmost Portuguese possession was Timor and Solor. Both islands were only partly occupied by the Portuguese, who respected the small native kingdoms and tribal rulers, under the superficial cover of Portuguese sovereignty. Timor depended on Macao and on the intensity of her trade relations with China.

CONSTITUTIONAL MONARCHY

The triumphs of Liberalism in Portugal were preceded by an unsuccessful conspiracy, the goals of which seemed to be more political than ideological. The Portuguese felt abandoned by their monarch; they complained about the heavy sums of money shipped yearly to Brazil in the form of rents and taxation along with the commercial decline and the unbalanced budget. In addition, the Portuguese resented the British influence in the army and the regency. In 1817, several people were arrested on the charge of plotting against marshal Beresford's life, the government and the existing institutions. A short trial brought death at the stake to a dozen people, including the alleged leader of the conspiracy, lieutenant-general Gomes Freire de Andrade.

The military revolted in Porto (August 24, 1820) and in a few days claimed full sovereignty in the north. Its main goals were to take over the regency and to summon the *cortes* with the aim of adopting a constitution. A second uprising (September 15), this time in Lisbon, ousted the rulers. The great names of the revolution were Fernandes Tomás, Ferreira Borges and Silva Carvalho, all jurists and bureaucrats.

The new government promoted elections for the *cortes*, which took place in December. A majority of bourgeois, landowners, traders and bureaucrats was elected, and requested that the king return to Portugal. John VI arrived in Lisbon in July 1821 after having sworn to uphold the future constitution. It is true that he appointed predominantly conservative ministers but, on the whole and for two years, he behaved well as a first constitutional monarch. The leaders of the absolutist movement were to be found rather in Queen Carlota Joaquina and her son, Prince Miguel.

The independence of Brazil (September 1822) inflicted a mortal blow to the liberal *cortes* and made the Liberals highly unpopular. Also, many of the innovations met with the resistance of the great majority of the people, who did not understand them, not to mention the clergy and the nobility. Under these circumstances, it was relatively easy for the anti-Liberal party to rise up in arms at the small town of Vila Franca and proclaim the restoration of absolutism (*Vilafrancada*, May 1823). John VI promised a new and better constitution to the country, while dissolving the *cortes* to please the victors.

Displeased, the extremist right-wing movement led by Miguel and his mother revolted once more in April 1824 *(Abrilada)*. John VI sought protection aboard an English man-of-war and, from there, backed by England, he forced Miguel into submission. The prince left the country, and the Moderate Absolutist regained power.

John's death (March 1826) posed a difficult problem. His eldest son, Pedro, was the emperor of Brazil. Thus, Pedro, acclaimed in Portugal as Pedro IV as soon as his father died, promptly abdicated on behalf of his daughter, Maria da Glória — then a child of seven — provided that she married her uncle Miguel, who would take over the regency of the kingdom. At the same time, Pedro granted Portugal a highly-conservative constitution *(Carta Constitucional)*.

Returning home (March 1828), Miguel dissolved the *cortes* and summoned new ones according to the old style. They proclaimed him absolute king (July 1828). Violent persecutions against the liberals permeated Miguel's six-year reign. Thousands left the country, thousands more were arrested and kept in jail in the worst possible conditions, many were executed or murdered.

The island of Terceira (Azores) had revolted against Miguel (1828) and gallantly upheld the liberal cause. In Brazil, circumstances forced emperor Pedro I to abdicate on behalf of his son Pedro II (1831), which gave him full freedom of action. He left Brazil and went to England and France, assuming direct leadership of the liberal cause. Arriving at Terceira (March 1832), Pedro took over the regency and left for Portugal with an expedition formed by some 7 500 men. He landed in Portugal in July 1832, near Porto (Mindelo). Caught by surprise, the absolutist forces which protected the city retreated, and the Liberals entered Porto almost without bloodshed four days later.

The civil war had thus started on the mainland. The absolutists, after this first disorientation, rallied together and besieged Porto for more than a year. In June 1833, the Liberals decided to try a different port of landing, which might relieve the absolutist pressure on Porto. A maritime expedition under the command of the Duke of Terceira left Porto and, in a surprise operation, landed in the south, in the Algarve. Some days later, the liberal fleet (under the mercenary English commander Napier) completely defeated the absolutist men-of-war. The Duke of Terceira marched on, reaching the Tagus in less than a month. The absolutists were badly beaten off the coast of Lisbon and their government decided to evacuate the capital. A day later, Lisbon was occupied with little resistance (July 24, 1833). England and France formally recognized Pedro's government.

The civil war continued for some time more. Late in May 1834, Miguel and his partisans were compelled to lay down arms.

However, the end of the civil war did not mean stability at home. The liberals were plagued by internal division. Not used to constitutional practice, most statesmen tended toward a disguised dictatorship which brought them into almost-permanent conflict with the *cortes*. When Pedro died (September 1834) of tuberculosis, the *cortes* and the government preferred to declare fifteen-year-old Maria II of age.

The coservatives held the power until 1836. Palmela, Terceira and Saldanha, along with some moderates, controlled the government and tried to instill some order and inject some prosperity into a country utterly exhausted and still bleeding from a civil war. They had the full support of the foreign powers, who saw in them the warrants of an English type of constitutionalism, depending on loans from abroad and committed to paying them on time.

In the 1836 elections, the opposition won in several important places, among them Porto. When its representatives arrived in Lisbon, the city garrisons revolted with popular support and forced the government to resign (September 1836). A new government, with Passos Manuel as the leading figure, assumed power, abolished the Constitutional Charter, and enforced the Constitution of 1822. The elections that followed gave him a majority, which allowed him to draft a new constitution, more extreme than the Charter but far less so than that of 1822.

«*Septembrism*» lasted, theoretically, until 1842, but it tended to be less and less radical. Moreover, it had to fight constant attempts to restore the Charter, which weakened it. From 1839 on, the secretary of Justice, Costa Cabral (a former radical), practically controlled things, being regarded by the crown and the right as the best warrant of order and prosperity.

In February 1842, Costa Cabral himself restored the Charter in Porto in a bloodless *coup d'état*. Power was returned to the right, but this time under an able and authoritarian leader, who knew how to rule and make himself obeyed. «Cabralism» (from Cabral) emphasized order and economic development. As such, it set up a regime of repression in the country. But, unlike Miguel, Costa Cabral did not want to go back to the past. He rather fostered the development of Portugal in a progressive way, particularly in the fields of public works and administration. Because of that, many of his reforms endured.

Costa Cabral's despotism brought about the most terrible and enduring civil war between liberals. The *Maria da Fonte* revolution — also called *Patuleia* — put together several contradictory forces, including absolutists, radicals, moderates and even Chartists who were against Costa Cabral's ruthlessness and corruption. Its first phase lasted only a month (April-May 1846) and came to an end with the ousting of Costa Cabral from government. But the revolt started again in October, turning into a full-scale civil war. It lasted for eight months and its results were generally favourable to the rebels. Their final victory, however, would bring about Maria's abdication and a government controlled by radicals. Neither England nor Spain could accept that. The Lisbon government asked for foreign intervention. A Spanish army entered Portugal, while the English fleet blockaded Porto. At Gramido, the rebels were forced to sign a treaty (June 1847) according to the terms of which they could lay down arms honourably.

The imposed peace brought Costa Cabral and his partisans back, although in a more moderate, less violent form. Saldanha, who had held the power up to this point, became the main leader of the opposition. In April 1851, he revolted and was supported by a military uprising in Porto. He called his movement the «Regeneration of Portugal», his partisans becoming known henceforth as «Regenerators» *(Regeneradores)*. Cabral's government fell, and Queen Maria II was forced to entrust Saldanha with the task of forming a new cabinet.

The country was tired of so much political turmoil, and desired peace. The bourgeoisie, in particular, required a strong yet flexible government which could ensure tranquillity and economic expansion. Saldanha's prestige accounted for the former, Fontes Pereira de Melo's plans for developing Portugal ensured the latter. The period of idealism was over. The 1852 amendment to the constitution, along with a new electoral law, put a practical end to the division between Chartists and Septembrists and made the Charter acceptable to almost everyone. The industrial, financial and trade expansion of Portugal attuned the interests of industrialists, financiers, traders and rural landowners on several levels, gathering together upper, middle, and petty bourgeoisie for a common goal. From 1851 until the rise of the Republican Party in the 1880s and the 1890s, one could say there was no real «opposition» to the institutions in Portugal.

Queen Maria II died in 1853. The heir to the throne, Pedro, was not yet of age, a regency being assumed by his father, nominal King Fernando II. As king, Pedro V began ruling in 1855, but he died very young, of typhus, in 1861. His brother Luis succeeded him on the throne, and went down in history as a model constitutional monarch. His marriage to Maria Pia, the daughter of Victor Emmanuel II of Italy, strengthened the ties with that country and helped his popularity among the leftist anticlericals.

Portugal's internal policy during the reign of Pedro V and Luis I (1853-89) was one of relative calm in the general framework of economic expansion and prosperity for the ruling classes. Here and there, some minor crises shook the political order, but they were of no great significance.

The stability of the 1870s and 1880s was followed by a deep political, economic and financial crisis. The contradictions of the constitutional monarchy became evident to everyone. Its ideology no longer held any appeal for the younger generations. Instead, socialism and republicanism pointed a new way. The Spanish and French revolutions in the 1870s played an important part in the rise of a Portuguese political consciousness. Anticlericalism also played a major role in the shaping of an opposition.

King Luis I died in 1889, and the new monarch, Carlos I, intelligent but haughty, did not enjoy his father's popularity.

The crisis that would lead to the fall of the monarchy was provoked by the ultimatum that Great Britain delivered to Portugal in January 1890. According to its terms, the Portuguese had to give up their claims to a vast African territory connecting Angola with Mozambique. This ultimatum caused a national wave of indignation against England and a widespread movement against the monarchy and the king himself, who was accused of neglecting the overseas territories and of jeopardizing the nation's interests. There were some riots, and in January 1891 the first republican uprising took place in Porto. It failed, but for the first time it revealed the existence of a real threat to the established institutions.

Dias Ferreira's cabinet was able to solve the financial crisis and smooth over the situation once again. As a consequence, the old party system was reinstated. *Regeneradores* under Hintze Ribeiro and *Progressistas* under José Luciano de Castro succeeded each other up to 1906.

By 1906, the *cortes* had become an assembly for chicanery and personal debate. Obstruction to any government and filibustering were common practice. The two large parties did little to avoid the accusations of corruption, inefficiency and uselessness laid upon them. The Republicans made the best use possible of internal monarchical dissension to attack the regime. Having finally decided to interfere and take a more active part in politics, the king forced Hintze Ribeiro to resign and entrusted João Franco and his new party with the task of forming a new cabinet. The new premier first got the support of the *Progressistas*, but later lost it and decided to try the dictatorial way.

The consequences were disastrous for the regime: Franco had the overwhelming majority of the organized forces in the country against him. It had been made public that the royal family owed the government (i.e. the nation) important sums of money in the form of successive loans, which brought about a violent campaign against the monarchy. Violence and repression permeated Franco's second year in government. Consequently, on February 1, 1908, King Carlos and the heir to the throne, Prince Luís Filipe, were assassinated in Lisbon.

Acclaimed as Manuel II, Carlos's second son, the new monarch, a youth of eighteen, dismissed Franco and called upon a coalition government. The prevailing attitude was one of appeasement, in contrast with the fierceness of the fallen dictatorship. The Republicans were given more freedom than ever, and their influence among the people increased. In the municipal elections of 1908, they won in Lisbon, electing a municipal council 100 per cent their own. In the general elections of August 1910, they triumphed in Lisbon and in several other places. In a country like Portugal, where the weight of the capital was paramount to the nation's life, this meant the end for the constitutional monarchy. Indeed, on October 4, 1910, a military and popular revolution in Lisbon easily disbanded the last defenders of the throne, the Republic being proclaimed the following day. King Manuel and his family left the country, never to return.

•

Liberalism entered Portugal by way of French and English influences. Freemasonry played a leading role in disseminating it. Although known in Portugal from early days, it was only by the time of Prince John's regency that the number and activity of the Portuguese Freemasons started to trouble the government. Persecutions of all kinds prevented a smooth development of the Masonry, especially during and after the French invasions. In spite of that, its number grew. Several Freemasons and Masonry sympathizers founded the so-called *Sinédrio* (1818), a secret society which decisively contributed to subversion and actually organized the Revolution of 1820.

The ideology that triumphed in 1820 contained some of the international trends of Liberalism, but also a good many national tendencies, like a certain defence of protectionism and high tariffs against free trade with foreign countries; the development of technology, transport and communications; and an «agrarian reform» tending to dismember the huge *latifundia* in the hands of the crown and the religious orders. Portuguese Liberalism also acknowledged the nation as being «the union of all Portuguese in both hemispheres» (which justified its «colonial» policies, both in 1820-25 regarding Brazil, and later regarding Africa); all Portuguese were granted, at least in theory, equal rights and duties. Liberalism also triumphed because it posed as a restorer of the old «liberties» of the realm. The adoption of the traditional word *cortes* was symbolic of this.

The constitution of 1822 mainly followed the Spanish constitution of 1812, although with some changes and adaptations to Portuguese reality. It asserted the sovereignty of the nation and admitted the independence of the three powers — legislative, executive and judicial. In terms of law-making, the king had only the right of «suspended veto», i.e. the right to bring back to the *cortes*, once, any law that he disagreed with, explaining the reasons for his discordance.

This constitution did not last. It was too progressive and too democratic for its time. Suffrage for all male literates might be dangerous for the interests of landowners and important businessmen. It did not satisfy the nobility or the clergy (neither were they given any special prerogatives), or the king, whose powers were reduced to almost nothing. No wonder, then, that it lasted for less than one year in its first phase (October 1822 to June 1823), and then, on a provisional and theoretical basis, from September 1836 to April 1838.

The second Portuguese constitution (1826) bore the name of «Constitutional Charter» *(Carta Constitucional)* and was generally known as «The Charter». It closely followed the Brazilian text (which, in turn, was influenced by the French model). It protected hereditary nobility and its privileges, and public debt, in an effort to obtain the support of the aristocracy and bourgeoisie. Moreover, it introduced a number of anti-democratic innovations. The state powers became four, instead of three: legislative, moderating *(Poder Moderador),* executive and judicial. The first one was vested in the *cortes*, which were composed of two Houses, the elected Chamber of Deputies and the Chamber of Peers, appointed by the king for life and with the right of transmission to their heirs, including archbishops and bishops. The moderating power, which the Charter considered to be «the key of all political organization», belonged to the king who, as its head, could appoint the peers, summon the *cortes* and dissolve the Chamber of Deputies, appoint and dismiss the government, suspend magistrates, grant amnesties and pardons, and veto the laws passed in the *cortes*.

The Charter of 1826 pleased both the nobility and the secular clergy, as well as the landowners and the wealthy bourgeois. It also granted extensive powers to the king. For these reasons, it had all warrants of success and long rule. Indeed, after an initial brief period of almost two years (1826-28), it lasted from 1834 to September 1836, and then, again, from February 1842 until the proclamation of the Republic, on October 5, 1910. In all, it was upheld for 72 years.

The third Portuguese constitution lasted less than four years (April 1838 to February 1842). A compromise between the constitution of 1822 and the Charter, it reasserted that sovereignty rested upon the nation (not the king); suppressed the hereditary Chamber of Peers and replaced it with an elected Chamber of Senators; and accepted direct elections for the Chamber of Deputies, albeit with highly-restrictive conditions to qualify as a voter. The moderating power was abolished, but the king kept the right to dissolve the Chambers and veto the laws.

The 68 years of continuous validity of the Charter depended upon three amendments, which gave way to a more democratic system. Among other things, elections to the Chamber of Deputies became direct, and the voting capacity was enlarged.

From 1820 to 1852, with the exception of two brief periods (1822-23; 1836-42), all elections were indirect, and both the voters' and candidates' qualifications were considerably tightened, determined on an income basis. Such restrictions put parliamentary representation in the hands of landowners, traders and industrialists, and parliamentary voting in the hands of the middle-class, both rural and urban. The electoral law of 1852 kept the income qualification for voting and for being elected, but it made elections direct again. The law of 1878 greatly increased the number of voters, by reducing the voting age from 25 to 21. The trend toward a more democratic basis was further enhanced in 1884, when a new law introduced the system of incomplete lists of candidates, which accounted for a much more proportional representation.

After 1851, two large parties were slowly created and alternated in power, the Regenerating Party and the Historical Party. Ideologically, they hardly differed. In uncompromising opposition, the Republican and the Socialist parties emerged, both in the 1870s, the former with a tremendous appeal to the popular masses, particularly in the towns. There were also new groups (resultant from dissensions). The most prominent new party was the «Regenerating-Liberal» Party of João Franco (in power between 1906 and 1908).

The secret and religious societies provided the framework for much political activity. Freemasonry was the most relevant among those societies, its action increasing in the early 1900s and becoming almost thoroughly republican-oriented. More popular and active was the Carbonary *(Carbonária)*, also arising at the beginning of the 20th century.

Theoretically, the great parties of the monarchy were organized upon the basis of local, freely-elected centres. As a matter of fact, such centres existed only in the towns. Elsewhere, and even in many towns, the party leader was the local chieftain, who controlled everything and everyone. Power did not emanate from the people to the parties and from the latter to the crown, but from the crown to the parties and from the latter to the local chieftain organizations. The people voted as they were ordered by whoever paid the most for votes. Public opinion was inconsequential and existed only in a few towns. Elections were «made» by the government, which always won them by means of a network of local authorities.

•

The opening of Brazilian ports to all nations in 1808, the commercial treaty with England in 1810 and the final independence of Brazil in 1822 ruined the foundations of Portuguese economy. When the bourgeois dreams of recovering the lost colony were over, and complete autonomy of former Portuguese America was acknowledged by the Treaty of Rio de Janeiro (1825), a new economic setting for Portugal had to be realistically envisaged.

No development of agriculture would be possible — so the physiocrats and the liberals contended — without complete destruction of «feudal» ties. Thus, the ecclesiastical tithe was abolished. The sales tax was reduced by half and maintained only on real estate. All feudal rights and other seigniorial traditions were abolished, like game preserves and stud farms. The so-called crown patrimony *(Bens da Coroa)* became the «Nation's patrimony» *(Bens Nacionais)*. Entailed property was also limited to wealthy estates. The numerous duties of all sorts existing in the borough charters *(forais)* were also abolished, as well as many internal tools on trade and circulation, import and export permits, and all hindrances to free commerce. Finally, lands to be cleared or recently cleared were granted freedom of taxation for a period of 20 years.

Another important act eliminated the religious orders (1834), and their property was conveyed out of mortmain and auctioned off. The government also sold much of the land belonging to the crown. In this way, previously wasted or improperly cultivated land now became productive, as this was in the interest of the new proprietors. The total suppression of entailed estates in 1863 gave property in Portugal a modern structure. Rural credit was also organized. Finally, the development of transportation and communications after 1840 brought about the beginning of adequate infrastructure for general economic progress.

The study of Portugal's empty lands throughout the 19th and early-20th centuries is the best proof of the country's development in agriculture and settlement. In 1819, two-thirds of Portuguese soil lay uncultivated; this had decreased to one-half 50 years later, and to less than 40 per cent in 1902.

Among the new crop cultures introduced or developed in this period, potatoes and rice were paramount, with important consequences. Potatoes replaced the extensive consumption of turnips and chestnuts in people's diets, particularly in the north and the northeast. At the beginning of the 20th century, rice production was intensified, gradually becoming a popular food for all Portuguese. Cork too was extensively developed, increasing its export by 100 per cent. With only a few exceptions, all forms of agriculture made remarkable progress. On the other hand, countless vines were destroyed by a disease, phylloxera, after 1842.

The development of industry was another feature of constitutional Portugal. A law abolished corporations and other hindrances to free growth of trade and industry (1834). Pre-capitalist forms of production and industrial relationships gradually evolved toward fully-capitalist forms. There were less than 15 thousand workers in 1 031 factories in 1822; 180 thousand in 1 350 factories in 1881; some 200 thousand in over five thousand factories on the eve of World War I. The textile industry had become the main source of income, followed by tobacco, milling, ceramics, cork and glass. Foreign capital began to enter Portugal at a quickening pace. By 1900, foreign firms had increased to one-sixth of the total, and their investments controlled one-fourth of Portugal's trade and industry. In 1891, the tobacco industry was converted into a monopoly, the capital of which belonged predominantly to foreigners.

The economic expansion of Portugal resulted largely from the governmental policy of developing transportation and communications, known as *Fontismo* (after statesman Fontes). Road and railroad building increased spectacularly and the first trains were in operation after 1856. Along with road and railroad expansion was bridge building. A large number of bridges were built, some of which were truly impressive. Railroad communication with Spain — and thus with Europe — opened in the 1860s.

Railroads were followed by telegraph, submarine cable and telephone. Wireless telegraph arrived at the beginning of the 20th century. Around the same time, the first tramcars appeared in the main cities. Harbours and lighthouses were greatly improved. In the 1890s, efforts to bring light to the Portuguese coastline (dubbed the «black coast») led to fruitful results with the building of numerous lighthouses.

In trade, the adoption of the liberal ideology prevented government's direct interference. It was, however, possible for the state to endow commerce with a framework that could regulate, organize and also simplify the free circulation and distribution of products. Private associations of all sorts for trade purposes resulted from these laws and the general economic expansion of the country. By 1875, some 15 commercial associations existed in the main urban centres, having an important impact on the rise of trade, industry, agriculture and overseas expansion.

The balance of trade registered a permanent deficit. At the beginning of the 20th century, Portugal imported (mainly from England) twice as much as she exported. The deficit could partly be covered by the foreign exchange credits sent by Portuguese immigrants in Brazil.

The rise to power of the bourgeoisie and the economic expansion of Portugal coincided with the foundation of the first banks. In 1821, new economic and social conditions enabled the establishment of the Bank of Lisbon, which was granted the monopoly of issuing banknotes. Many other banks appeared afterwards, strictly connected with the economic and financial cycles. There were 28 banks in 1910.

The end of Brazil as a colony and the abolition of many feudal taxes reduced revenue, while the French invasions, revolutions, civil wars and structural reforms hopelessly increased expenditure. Later, the very expansion of Portugal brought about new state expenses in all areas. Consequently, both the budget deficit and public debt grew larger and larger. Fontism, along with the general development of the country and the end of the revolutionary period, eased the budgetary situation. In the 1850s, revenues permanently surpassed the level of 1805 and jumped forward rapidly. At the beginning of the 20th century, Portugal, in terms of taxation, was five times wealthier than at the apogee of her exploitation of Brazil, a clear proof that the country could survive even without colonies (in those days, public revenue derived from the colonies was minimal).

Among the structural changes which shaped a new Portugal, the reforms in administration were significant. They closely followed the French law, in those days considered the most perfect example. According to the constitutional principles, administrative and judicial functions could not and should not be confused, as they had been before. Thus, the new laws thoroughly changed most of the existing rules on administration. The seesaw policy between centralization and decentralization would, in fact, permeate its history. The Azores and Madeira islands resisted the trend toward greater centralization, fighting for local autonomy. This battle was won in 1895 (Azores) and 1901 (Madeira), when they achieved some administrative autonomy.

In government, the growing complexity of public affairs led to an increase in the number of secretariats and internal departments. Other reforms encompassed the army and the navy, welfare and, of course, the overseas territories.

Population grew from 3 300 000 in the 1820s, to 4 200 000 in 1864, and almost 6 million in 1911. Lisbon was home to some 210 thousand people in 1820, a figure that remained almost static until the 1860s. The great leap forward started then: 301 206 in 1890, and 434 436 in 1911. Together, Lisbon and Porto encompassed more than 11 per cent of the country's population, in contrast with eight per cent 90 years before. The trend toward a continuous rise in population in the coastal regions and a stagnation or decrease in the rest of the country went on, undisturbed, until the late-1800s. Another important trait of demographical evolution was the increasing immigration to America, particularly to Brazil, after 1850.

Among the fundamental changes in structure carried out by the liberal governments after 1820, religious reform should not be omitted. The *cortes* began by abolishing the Inquisition. This abolition had a symbolic meaning, because the Inquisition had been slowly fading away for years. Much more important was the attitude toward the religious orders which would be abolished in 1834, in part because the great majority of the regular clergy sided with the absolutist opposition. On the other hand, the constitution of 1826 favoured the secular clergy. Bishops had been granted permanent representation in the upper chamber, which put them on the same level as the high nobility. Paradoxically, their subordinates at the head of the parishes also started to receive some economic benefits from the triumph of the new order, based upon equality and governmental subsidies, because most of the existing revenue had, until then, been given to bishops and to the regular clergy. The dissolution of the religious orders brought no particular harm to the country. Socially, it met with little resistance and was applauded or accepted with indifference by most people, including the secular clergy. As a matter of fact, the religious orders came back, although much more moderately, after the 1850s. A law of 1901 practically authorized the coming of any religious order to Portugal provided it pursued educational or charitable goals.

The other pillar of absolutism, the feudal nobility, suffered comparatively less than the clergy. The law abolished feudal rights and commanderies and also entailed property, deprived the nobles of their usual allowances granted by the king, nationalized crown property, and so forth. To subsist, the nobles had to rely exclusively upon their own estates and their participation in trade and industry. This moved them closer to the bourgeoisie than ever before. On the other hand, the constitution of 1826 granted the nobility hereditary representation in the upper chamber, one of the reasons why it could triumph and subsist — despite its multiple changes — to the end of the monarchy. The government policy of granting titles to petty aristocrats, traders, bureaucrats and military went on at a still more rapid pace. By the end of the century, old aristocracy and constitutional aristocracy were so intermingled that it would have been difficult to distinguish between them through anything other than historical grounds.

The bourgeoisie, which had been given a large share in government and administration since Pombal, triumphed in 1820 and then, permanently, in 1834. Up until the beginning of the 20th century, it continued to grow. By the second half of the century, the bourgeoisie undoubtedly increased in class-consciousness. Titles of nobility became less coveted and were sometimes even refused.

Among the lower ranks of society, the main change was the slow and gradual rise of a proletariat. Early in the 19th century, craft workers who owned their shop and tools in the old style of production still made up two-thirds of the whole «industrial population». Rural workers, however, who owned little or nothing, constituted some 70 per cent of the total rural population. A century later, there were 100 thousand workers in factories with more than ten people — i. e. real proletarians —, some 20 per cent of the total number of workers engaged in industry and craft activities. The great majority of the «industrial» population were still working in small shops and in craft activities at home. General working conditions seem to have worsened during the 19th century. Real salaries decreased, standards of living, nutrition and lodging also worsened. Neither the government nor the industrialists provided the workers with any legal protection or assistance against accidents, old age, and the like.

Workers responded in one of two ways: by joining associations and by striking. A Socialist Party appeared in the 1870s, and its role in the life of the country began to have a certain relevance after the turn of the century.

Despite these and other factors, the proletariat in Portugal in the early-20th century didn't pose a threat to the bourgeois leadership. Proletarians generally appeared as the humble clients of traders, industrialists and landowners, with a strong clerical influence to divert them from any widespread rebellion.

The liberal revolution fostered glamorous principles of providing education to all citizens. The Constitutional Charter established free primary education as a right. After 1834, progress in all fields of education could be carried out without interruption. The number of official primary schools steadily increased.

Accordingly, the rate of illiteracy gradually declined, down to 69,7 per cent in 1911. However, these figures still seemed quite high, a fact which endowed Republican propaganda with one of its best arguments.

The ruling classes of Liberalism were actually more concerned with the two upper levels of education. One of their major achievements was the thorough reform of secondary studies, according to the French pattern of the Lycée (1836), and the introduction of secondary technical studies.

By comparison, university education reform was poor. Coimbra continued its theoretical monopoly of university studies. The only significant alterations in almost a century were the fusion of the two schools of Law and Canons into one and the addition of a few scientific subjects. The development of university studies in 19th-century Portugal was more prominent in the other schools which were gradually created in Lisbon and Porto: the Polytechnical Schools, the Schools of Medicine and Surgery, the Military Academy, the Naval School, the General Conservatory of Dramatic Art, the Schools of Fine Arts, and the Upper Institute of Letters.

One of the most interesting features of 19th-century Portugal was cultural development, a result of opening the country to outside influences, abolishing censorship, and stimulating discussion on all levels and on almost all subjects. The legislation of 1836-37 provided the framework for the development of Portuguese theatre, which was best represented by Almeida Garrett (1799-1854). History experienced tremendous development, with the systematic use of archival sources. Alexandre Herculano showed incomparable talent for history, the concept of which he entirely remodelled according to the modern principles of his time. The novel developed in Portugal in accordance with the new social conditions and also because of the influence of French and English authors. A first generation of Romantics (Camilo Castelo Branco, Júlio Dinis) supplied the basis for the exceptionally-realistic novels of Eça de Queirós (1845-1900) and some other lesser-known contemporaries of his.

Eça de Queirós belonged to the «generation of 1870», a remarkable group of intellectuals who flourished from the late-1870s to the beginning of the 20th century. They were the result of Portugal's complete openness, enabled by the development of communications and a free press. They were the exponents of the new Portugal, European-minded, modern, striving to rise from industrial, commercial and political underdevelopment to a new society based on the industrial revolution, bourgeois leadership and the parliamentary system. The Portuguese generation of 1870 was anticlerical, rationalist, positivist (or, at least, strong believers in scientism) and generally anti-monarchist, some of their members tending toward a Republican system, others even aiming at vague socialism.

In the field of science, Portugal played a much more modest role. Modern science required more extensive equipment and costly devices which were generally out of reach of the meagre budgets of schools and governments. Nonetheless, countless efforts led to the opening of many scientific museums, laboratories, observatories and botanical gardens, and to a moderate flourishing of science which, if not inventive, at least managed to keep up with the international scientific movement.

AFRICA

In the 19th century, central and southern Africa began to be influenced by the growth of European settlement and expansion. One expedition after another left the coastal areas of Angola and Mozambique with varied purposes and uneven achievements. These explorations made known to Europe vast territories between latitude 7° and 27° S, and were instrumental in promoting European settlement not only in Portuguese but also in British areas — in present-day Zambia, Malawi, Zimbabwe and Zaire.

Navy Commanders Hermenegildo Capelo and Roberto Ivens left in 1877 for their first exploration, which took them to Bié in 1888. Their report, a fine piece of geographical knowledge, was widely publicized. A former companion of theirs, Captain Serpa Pinto, undertook the crossing of Africa from west to east. From Bié (1877), Serpa Pinto travelled south, to central Zambia. He continued further south via the Zambezi River, and then proceeded all the way south to Pretoria (Transvaal) and Durban (1879), becoming the first Portuguese and one of the first Europeans to cross the entire African continent. He wrote a famous account of his expedition, published just after the deed.

Capelo, Ivens and Serpa Pinto undertook other voyages too. The first two departed from Moçâmedes (south Angola), crossing, again, the continent, all the way to Quelimane (1884-85). Accompanied by Augusto Cardoso, Serpa Pinto also travelled in Mozambique, going from the town of Mozambique on the coast, north to Ibo, and then west to Lake Nyassa.

These were only the most famous among many other expeditions undertaken by traders, officers and scientists, within the present boundaries of Angola and Mozambique, which definitely helped make available better geographical knowledge of both colonies. The elaborate maps of the late-19th and early-20th centuries came as a direct result, as well as having fostered interest in trade projects among both blacks and whites. Numerous map committees, geographical missions and military operations completed the basic tasks started by the explorers of the mid-19th century.

By 1830 or 1840, the Portuguese effective occupation of Angola was limited to a narrow strip of coastal territory. In Mozambique, the Portuguese controlled even less territory than in Angola. From Cape Delgado to Lourenço Marques, even the occupation of the coastline was not continuous. Only along the Zambezi River was there deep penetration inland, for the Portuguese were well settled down to Tete and beyond, nearly 500 kilometres (320 miles) from the coast. In Guinea, Portuguese authority was limited to some fortresses and villages not necessarily connected by other than coastal navigation. The situation in distant Timor was similar.

The various attempts to officially promote colonization in Africa did not meet with great success. Emigrants preferred Brazil or the United States, where well-organized societies needed them and promptly provided them with jobs and high salaries. By the early-19th century, there were, throughout the Portuguese «empire», less than 10 thousand Europeans. Cape Verde, Angola and India absorbed the largest number, a great many of whom were banished outcasts and garrison men. Even the garrisons included a large majority of Africans and Asians under the command of white Portuguese officers.

After the middle of the century, things started changing, but not much. Angola housed only some 12 thousand Europeans when the Republic was proclaimed, and Mozambique was home to only half of that number. «Towns» were little more than villages, with some few exceptions: Macao (78 thousand), Pangim (Goa), Luanda and Lourenço Marques — none of the three exceeding 20 thousand inhabitants in 1910, all races included.

Tribal differentiation, rivalries and frequent warfare always prevented the African peoples in contact with the Portuguese from uniting themselves against the common foe. Except for very brief periods of sporadic «empires», i.e. confederation of tribes under a prestigious leader (like the Zulu Tusi or Watutsi empire, in south Mozambique), the Portuguese had relatively little trouble in imposing their sovereignty, whenever they were determined to do it. When peaceful means were insufficient or proved useless, so-called «campaigns of submission» took place. Few as they were, they often depended upon individual deeds, daring prowesses, and the like, which had a deep impact on the minds of Africans.

The Portuguese system of colonization — whenever it existed — always aimed at converting the African into a Portuguese. Teaching was to be in Portuguese and only Portuguese was accepted as the official language; religion and morals were to be Christian and, if possible, Roman Catholic; customs, traditions and way of life were to relate to the Portuguese fatherland, not to the African past. Consequently, learning and preservation of African languages and cultures could only be envisioned from a strictly scientific standpoint or as a provisional bridge for communication between whites and blacks.

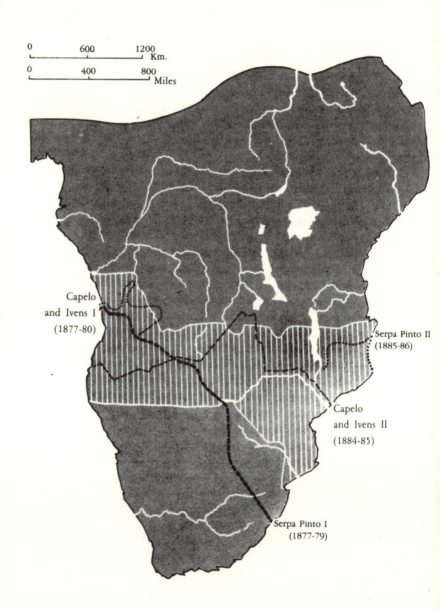

The question of slavery hovered over the entire Portuguese colonial administration until the 20th century. Following the Treaty of Vienna (1815), England and Portugal signed an agreement to curb the slave trade in the Portuguese possessions. Portugal pledged to supress it north of the equator, which meant her colonies of Cape Verde and Guinea. Yet, easy as such measures seemed in theory, their practical application met with insuperable obstacles. In fact, slave trade was the only source of prosperity for colonies like Guinea and Angola. The Brazilian demand for slaves was a temptation that few would resist. For a long time, enforcement of the anti-slavery policy appeared hopeless. Indeed, it succeeded only with the final abolition of slavery in Brazil in 1888.

The treaty of 1842 between Portugal and Great Britain completely abolished all forms of slave trade in the overseas possessions of both countries. Enlightened public opinion in Portugal pressured the government to carry out abolition, by declaring all slaves free. After a period of transition, the law of February 25, 1869 reduced it, by declaring an immediate end to slavery in every corner of the Portuguese empire. However, it kept the existing slaves as freed-men *(libertos)*, compelled to provide services to their former lords. When the *libertos* disappeared, the *serviçais* (servants) came into existence according to the new code of native labour. There were differences between slaves, freedmen and servants, but only to a minor degree. Clearly, total freedom for many Africans was still far away. A kind of disguised slavery thus appeared, with highly-different aspects from area to area, but particularly conspicuous as far as the export of labour to the São Tomé plantations and to the South African mines were concerned. The Portuguese administration tried to correct some of the abuses, which it acknowledged: it promoted the hiring of Africans from other parts under improved and better-controlled contracts; it corrected several injustices and published a new labour code; it ordered an inquiry and salary increases, etc.

The lack of developed ecclesiastical organization and the shortage of clerics also hampered the Portuguese advance in Africa. To the end of the Monarchical period, there were few signs of a missionary revival in the overseas territories. The extinction of the religious orders (1834) was behind the permanent lack of missionaries, during the whole of the 19th century, in spite of the fact that the picture was already dismal long before. In the East, the Portuguese rights of patronage were constantly violated by the Holy See through the *Propaganda Fide* organization, simply because the Portuguese were no longer able to promote effective Christianization of India or China.

•

The Constitution of 1822 defined the Portuguese nation as «the union of all Portuguese of both hemispheres», encompassing Portugal proper, the Atlantic islands, Brazil and the African and Asian possessions, which were clearly and carefully listed. No distinction was made between whites and blacks, or between Portuguese from Portugal and Portuguese born in the overseas territories. The legislators of 1822 were obviously thinking of Brazil or India rather than Africa. Yet the principle had been established and similar definitions and descriptions were included in all the Constitutional Charters, despite the growing annexation of African peoples who were thoroughly strange to Portuguese culture.

The legislation of 1820-22 went further still. All matters relating to the colonies began to be dealt with by each of the departments of Portugal, together with the Portuguese affairs.

This utopia, which brought about considerable disorganization of public services in Africa and Asia, came to an end in 1835. The Secretariat of Navy and Overseas *(Marinha e Ultramar)* was revived. To assist it, the constitutional monarchy re-established an Overseas Council *(Conselho Ultramarino)*. In 1868, its name was changed to *Junta Consultiva do Ultramar,* and its powers considerably reduced.

In terms of legislation and its practical application to the overseas territories, the 19th-century tendency was never far from excessive centralization. Laws for the African and Asian colonies would result from decisions taken at *cortes*. Executive government, however, had the power to legislate whenever urgency or simple interruption of parliamentary sessions required it. Local governors were given local emergency powers too, but later acts curbed them so much that Lisbon actually had to be consulted in every respect.

The Portuguese administrative, civil, and criminal codes, as well as other European types of legislation, were applied to Africa and Asia with few adjustments to the local usages and traditions. In 1836, «general» and «particular» governments *(governos gerais* and *governos particulares)* were established for the overseas «dominions». A council *(Conselho de Governo)* was to assist each governor-general. This system lasted until 1869, when a new reform somewhat increased decentralization by granting the governors larger powers and stimulating local initiatives through the newly-created general juntas *(juntas gerais)*. Later changes separated Guinea from Cape Verde, in 1879, and Timor from Macao in 1863-66. Electoral representativeness existed from the very beginning of the constitutional regime. In most cases, representatives were simply «appointed» by Lisbon, and often among people who had few connections with the electoral district, rather than being chosen by the settlers. Yet some exceptions and real electoral struggle could occasionally be noted.

Up to the 1850s, and even afterwards, most of the Portuguese colonial economy rested upon slavery. With few exceptions, the estimates of other exports showed poor agricultural or industrial development.

Fontism and, to a certain extent, Cabralism before it, attempted to establish in the overseas dominions, albeit in a much moderate way, what was being tried at home, i.e. the development of infrastructures as a means of promoting trade and agriculture. Yet the overseas territories always depended upon the economic and financial situation in Portugal proper.

Railroad building, involving huge capital, many labourers, skilled leadership and military protection took a long time to develop and never achieved satisfactory levels. The first railroad track attempted to connect Lourenço Marques with Transvaal, giving northern South Africa easy access to the sea. Begun in 1870, it rapidly became one of the most significant railroads in all of Africa. The next railway line was built in Goa, connecting the port of Mormugão to British India. In 1887, a new track began to be built in Mozambique — with the purpose of connecting Beira to present-day Zimbabwe — as well as the first one in Angola, which connected Luanda with the country's inland. The development of maritime communications with the mainland went along with better equipment of harbours and other facilities, and the building of lighthouses.

From an agricultural standpoint, the great wonder was for a long time São Tomé and Príncipe. By the early-20th century, the two islands were regarded as a model colony and were proudly displayed to the world as a proof of Portuguese colonial capacities. This economic «miracle» was attributable to the well-managed coffee and cacao plantations *(roças)*, served by cheap labour and relatively-good trade facilities. At the time of the proclamation of the Republic, São Tomé and Príncipe were among the three world's greatest cacao producers. A sort of equatorial botanical garden, the two islands also nurtured many other exotic products. The plantations and the islands' trade belonged mostly to Portuguese absentee landlords.

Agriculture was not as successful in every other Portuguese colony. In Angola, for instance, despite all the efforts carried out until the beginning of the century, rubber, by far the most profitable export, reached only about one-third to one-half the value of São Tomé's cacao. Mozambique's agriculture, on the rise since the 1890s, could not compete with São Tomé's either.

In Mozambique, the need for rapid development after 1890 brought about the establishment of chartered companies, some of which acted like states within the state: the Mozambique Company, the Nyasa Company, the Zambezia Company, along with several other societies, appeared in the 1890s and early-1900s for agricultural and mining activities.

The cultural development of all Portuguese overseas provinces was slow throughout the whole period. Although education reforms tried to do something for the colonies, primary education was established very slowly in the various provinces. Secondary education started in Goa, where the first *liceu* (high-school) was opened. In the other colonies, however, no *liceus* existed until the 1890s (Macao) and the 1900s. Technical schools appeared in the 1870s and the 1880s in Goa, Angola and Mozambique, but much later (1900s) in places like Cape Verde and São Tomé. As for university studies, only Science and Medicine would flourish, and only in Portuguese India.

A printing press developed very slowly in each of the Portuguese territories (with the exception of India and

Macao) throughout the 19th century. The first local newspapers appeared, but with little continuity and poor editing. In every colony, the most important newspaper was always the administration gazette, called «Official Bulletin» *(Boletim Oficial)*, which often included general news and even literary subjects.

In Lisbon, and elsewhere in Portugal, scientific interest in Africa developed considerably in the mid- and late-19th century. In 1851, the government entrusted the Austrian botanist Dr. Friedrich Welwitsch with the mission of studying the flora of Angola. His counterpart for the fauna of Angola was the Portuguese scientist José de Anchieta, who started his expeditions to Africa in 1864. The foundation of the *Lisbon Geographical Society* (1875) had a decisive impact on the studies of tropical geography, ethnography, anthropology, history, botany, zoology, geology and other related sciences.

By the late-19th and early-20th centuries, several government-sponsored services were also established to carry out research and promote knowledge in the overseas territories. They were particularly active in geology, meteorology, veterinary science and hydrography. Scientific expeditions were dispatched to Africa, like those devoted to research and to combatting sleeping sickness. In 1902, an *Institute for Tropical Medicine,* including a school and a hospital, was opened in Lisbon, quickly ranking among the best in Europe. A school for colonial affairs also appeared in the nation's capital by the early-20th century.

•

The political history of Portuguese Africa and Asia throughout this period was marked by intense diplomatic activity to maintain and enlarge the existing territories, as well as no less intense warfare to occupy them permanently.

North of the equator, both the French and the British threatened the Portuguese claims and actual occupation of the coast of Guinea. Along the coast of Angola, British and French claims also threatened the Portuguese interests and led to some loss of effective sovereignty.

On the east coast, England and Germany posed the main threats. For a long time, England tried very hard to oust the Portuguese from the Lourenço Marques area, realizing the tremendous importance of that harbour for the economic development of inland Africa on the same latitude. In the extreme north of Mozambique, the border settlement did not go unquestioned. The Germans had occupied present-day Tanzania (Tanganyika) and, in 1894, they landed on the southern bank of the Rovuma River, and replaced the few Portuguese authorities with German ones, extending their occupation to a sort of triangular area (generally called Kionga).

Yet the main problem for Portugal, which preoccupied successive governments, and the one where her efforts failed completely, concerned inland tropical Africa, connecting Angola and Mozambique. The international conference in Berlin (1884-85) drafted a «General Act», which defined «a new colonial public law». Therefore, effective occupation replaced historical rights and forced the Portuguese to display a quick and impossible effort in order to send troops and public officials to all the areas which they claimed as theirs. From 1885 to 1890, the Portuguese organized several expeditions and tried to promote the effective occupation of the territories between the two coasts. It was, of course, too late. Lisbon became lost in theoretical dreams of establishing a large empire, which, by its very shape, conflicted with the British imperial plans. In 1887, the Portuguese Foreign Minister, Henrique Barros Gomes, presented to the House of Deputies a map of «Portuguese Meridional

Africa» in which Angola and Mozambique were connected. As the possessions were coloured pink, this map became known as the «Pink Map» *(Mapa cor de rosa)*. It gave Portugal almost all of Zambia, Malawi and Zimbabwe.

Several expeditions were planned, and Major Serpa Pinto was entrusted with studying the area for a future railroad connecting Lake Nyasa and the eastern coast. Relations between Portugal and England deteriorated quite rapidly and, on January 11, 1890, Lord Salisbury's government sent an ultimatum to Portugal requiring the immediate withdrawal of all Portuguese forces active in the contested areas. The alternative was a breakdown in diplomatic relations, very likely to result in the use of force.

Facing the threat of war, the Portuguese complied with the British demands, and withdrew. A first treaty, signed by the governments of both countries in August 1890 (Hintze Ribeiro as Foreign Minister), was rejected by the Portuguese parliament and by people in general. Only in June 1891 was the final treaty ratified. Slightly worse for the Portuguese interests than the rejected one, it nonetheless gave Portugal some territories where the Portuguese had never set foot. In May, another treaty, this time including the «Congo Free State», acknowledged a new and vast area in Angola, east of the Cuango River, as Portuguese. Paradoxically, by replacing a well-defined country of nearly 800 thousand square miles with a vague, unoccupied, and only historically-claimed territory, the treaties of 1891 granted Portugal an empire — the third in her history — almost as large as Brazil had ever been under effective Portuguese occupation.

In the Far East, Portugal's problems could be solved more easily. In India, Britain recognised the borders of Goa, Damão and Diu as defined in the 18th century. In Timor, treaties with Holland in 1851-59 sold the Portuguese rights to Solor and the island of Flores, and defined the border between the Dutch and the Portuguese sides of Timor.

Border definition did not stop the greediness of the big powers where the Portuguese colonies were concerned. The Anglo-German convention of 1898 foresaw an economic partition of Angola, Mozambique and Timor between the two countries. The outbreak of the Boer War (1899) brought Great Britain and Portugal closer together again. By a secret treaty signed at Windsor in October of that year, Great Britain pledged to recognise and guarantee the territorial integrity of Portugal and her colonies, while Portugal undertook to allow British troops to go through Mozambique on their way to Transvaal. Yet a new Anglo-German treaty about Portugal's colonies was negotiated in 1913, more as a provisional appeasing policy on England's side than as a real menace to Portugal. On the eve of World War I, the Germans openly uttered their imperialistic designs over Angola, Mozambique and other colonies. Portugal's intervention in the war on the side of the allies definitely saved the African empire for the Portuguese, until the onset of independence movements.

The internal history of Angola, Mozambique and Guinea up until the beginning of the 20th century was one of constant warfare, marked by the successful, though difficult Portuguese undertaking of subduing African tribes. Of the three, however, Mozambique proved, if not the most difficult to subdue, at least the one where military operations had a larger scope and where colonial heroes displayed their greatest deeds. In the south, the Portuguese faced a well-organised African state, the so-called Vátua «empire» led by Gungunhana. In the 1890s, Vátua attacks on Lourenço Marques caused much fear in the white Europeanised population. Royal commissioner António Enes prepared a systematic campaign against the Vátuas with great care, which was successful. In a daring feat, Mousinho de Albuquerque reached the Vátua capital, Chimite, and arrested Gungunhana (1895). Attempts at Mozambique's subjugation continued throughout the late-1890s and early-1900s, right up until the eve of World War I.

THE FIRST REPUBLIC

Once in power, the Republican party set up a provisional government symbolically headed by the aged and respected professor Teófilo Braga; the actual leaders, however, were the secretaries of the Interior (António José de Almeida), Justice (Afonso Costa) and, later, Public Works (Brito Camacho). In less than one year, this government achieved some of the main objectives of the republican programme, as well as tranquillity inside the country and international recognition of the new regime. In a conservative and predominantly monarchist Europe, the position of the Portuguese Republic was difficult and dangerous. This explains the concern for order and tolerance that, above all, led the efforts of the government. Many revolutionary initiatives were slowed down or simply forgotten, especially in the social area. And much of the sympathetic attitude towards the new regime faded away, especially among the working classes.

Rivalries and fights among the republicans came quickly. In the presidential elections which followed the approval of the constitution, the partisans of António José de Almeida and Brito Camacho succeeded in electing their candidate, old lawyer Manuel de Arriaga, instead of Afonso Costa's nominee, former university professor Bernardino Machado. Until January 1913, coalition cabinets ruled the country, with a plurality of Evolutionists (partisans of Almeida) and Unionists (partisans of Camacho). The new regime increasingly gained the nation's support. Several monarchical plots and attempts to foster civil war and the return of the king failed.

In January 1913, President Arriaga entrusted Afonso Costa with the task of organizing a cabinet of Democrats, the leading party. With the support of the Unionists in parliament, Afonso Costa and his group legislated intensely, balanced the budget, strengthened the government's authority and increased his popularity among the bourgeoisie. He lost it, however, among the lower classes by ruthlessly suppressing street demonstrations, discouraging strikes and sending many workers to prison. He also roused the hatred of the monarchists, the Church and the upper classes by repressing their plots and imprisoning their leaders.

Petty parliamentary quarrels and Arriaga's undiminished dislike of Afonso Costa brought about Costa's downfall a year later. The president called upon Bernardino Machado, who organized another cabinet, less democratic, yet supported by them. Up until January 1915, the Democratic Party ruled Portugal for all practical purposes.

Meanwhile, World War I had begun. It became clear to most people that Portugal's national interest was to join the allies. Both Democrats and Evolutionists agreed upon that. The Unionists, however, thought the opposite, or wanted to wait for a clearer picture of the war's outcome. Bernardino Machado's government made clear its intention of intervening in the struggle, but only if and when England required it.

Alarmed with the bitter political struggle and the gradual take-over by the Democrats, president Arriaga staged a coup in January 1915 and entrusted a personal friend of his, aged general Pimenta de Castro, with the difficult task of pacifying the country and presiding over impartial elections. The war policy was practically forgotten, persecutions against the monarchists and the Church stopped altogether (with many dismissed officers and civil servants being reinstated), and discrimination against the Democrats began. In March, army troops prevented parliament from assembling. In May 1915, a violent rebellion in Lisbon overthrew the government and reinstated the Democrats. President Arriaga resigned, old Teófilo Braga being sworn in as head of state. In August, regular presidential elections put Bernardino Machado in power for the 1915-1919 term. Afonso Costa regained the premiership.

Early in 1916, increasing problems in sea transportation led Great Britain to ask Portugal to seize a number of German merchant ships which had sought shelter in Portuguese harbours since the beginning of the war. When Portugal did seize these ships, Germany declared war on Portugal (March 9, 1916). The Democrats and the Evolutionists joined forces in a so-called Sacred Union *(União Sagrada)* and Afonso Costa stepped down from the premiership in favour of his old foe, António José de Almeida. For all practical purposes, however, the Democrats kept control of the situation, and Afonso Costa, as Finance Minister, had the final word in most important decisions. Later, a cabinet reshuffling restored the premiership to him.

The government undertook the difficult task of organizing an expeditionary force to fight in France, besides the various expeditions sent to Angola and Mozambique. At home, however, the war effort and the world's situation in general brought about disastrous results. Social unrest plagued the country, forcing the government to adopt severe measures of repression.

In December 1917, some Lisbon garrisons revolted with popular support, under the leadership of the former envoy to

Germany, major Sidónio Pais. The government surrendered, president Bernardino Machado was forced to leave the country, Afonso Costa was arrested and Sidónio Pais set up a military dictatorship. He changed the constitution, introduced a presidential regime in the American style, and had himself elected as president. His main support came from right-wing elements, including many monarchists.

Sidónio Pais's regime (called the «New Republic» — *República Nova*) was one of increasing confusion and terror. Though well-intentioned and skilled, enjoying immense popularity due to his gallant presence, boldness and demagogical attributes, Sidónio always lacked cadres to help him in complex tasks of administration and warfare. Social unrest went on undiminished. Many workers, who had trusted Sidónio Pais, now realized that his policies were the same, if not worse, than those pursued by the Democrats. The consequence of all this was repression. In December 1918, the president was assassinated, and Portugal was plunged into the worst crisis of her modern history.

The cabinet hastily had its dean, admiral Canto e Castro, elected president by the two Houses of Parliament and attempted a compromise with both left and right. The monarchists prepared the restoration of the regime deposed in 1910, proclaiming it in Porto and in Lisbon (January 1919).

It was relatively easy to staunch the uprising in the south. In the north, however, the monarchists held on, controlling a large part of the country. The civil war ended with the reinstatement of the Republican authorities in Porto (February 13, 1919). In March, a coalition government took power but it was one where the Sidonists no longer participated. General elections gave victory to the Democrats. Old party leader António José de Almeida was chosen as president (August 1919). For a better defence of the Republic, the Democrats had armed the

National Guard with artillery and granted it extensive powers. As a result, the National Guard practically made and unmade governments for the next two years.

In 1920 and 1921, corruption, political crime and lack of authority were, in Portugal as in many other countries in Europe, more rampant than ever. In 1920, seven governments succeeded each other. In October 1921, a radical rebellion brought down the cabinet. The following night, several well-known politicians were murdered. It seems that the crimes were not directly related to the rebellion, but to a mixture of elements where personal issues predominated, but where Rightist influences were present (the monarchists, the Church, even Spain were behind the scenes), aimed at bringing discredit to the regime.

In 1922, the National Guard was extensively disarmed and ceased to present any real danger. Only the army now showed a certain cohesion and prestige. Political fatigue made the years of 1922 and 1923 somewhat calmer, António Maria da Silva being able to head an all-Democratic cabinet for 21 months. The overall atmosphere tended to improve, along with the gradual fading of the war problems, although inflation continued. In August 1923, parliament elected the Democratic nominee, Manuel Teixeira Gomes, a writer and ambassador to London, as president.

Álvaro de Castro's government (1923-24) succeeded in putting an end to inflation and implementing some other interesting acts. But he was overthrown, as all the others, after a six-month administration. In November 1924, the left democrat José Domingues dos Santos presided over a three-month cabinet. This «Leftist» tendency collided with most of the Army, which showed its sympathies toward authoritarian regimes like Mussolini's in Italy and Primo de Rivera's in Spain. Two supressed army uprisings during 1925 clearly revealed such sympathies, also shared by monarchists, nationalists and other rightists. President Teixeira Gomes, constantly attacked by the Nationalists, resigned (December 1925), and old Bernardino Machado stepped in for his second term as president.

On May 28, 1926, general Gomes da Costa, one of the most prestigious war heroes, rebelled in the north (Braga) and marched towards the south. Most of the army joined him or accepted the coup.

In Lisbon, the government resigned (May 30), and the president entrusted one of the revolutionary leaders, Navy commander Cabeçadas, with the task of organizing a new cabinet. On May 31, Bernardino Machado himself resigned. Early in June, parliament was dissolved. The revolution had won.

•

Although a Republican ideology in Portugal can be traced back to 1820, it was only by the mid-19th century that it started to be clearly expressed and responded to. It called for a decentralized republic, socialist and federalist within a general federation of the Iberian peoples. It can be said that Portuguese Republicanism after 1858 simply developed and focussed its basic ideology, the only addition being anticlericalism. As a counterpart, however, it gradually lost the earlier socialist and federalist elements.

To become an ideology of the masses, as it certainly did become, Republicanism lost in constructivism and consistency, while gaining in destructionism and heterogeneity. In fact, in their final stage, Republican ideals were little different from those of 1820, which the constitutional monarchy had tried to interpret and apply in a pragmatic way. The Republic was thereby deprived of a great many practical achievements which had cemented and institutionalized the liberal monarchy, and almost reduced it to the difficult or impossible task of perfecting formulas already experimented with.

The basic structure of the Republican party system after 1910 encompassed a large and well-organized centre-left party — the Democratic Party —, and several marginal groups which were formed, developed, declined and faded according to circumstances and to the personalities who led them. The Democratic Party was organized into parish, municipal and district committees and ruled by a «Directory» elected by the Party Convention. Two small and more conservative parties arose in 1912, the Evolutionist and the Unionist. In 1919, as the two parties merged, a conservative party also came into existence, the Liberal Party. By 1923, the Liberal Party disbanded and tried to reorganize its forces under a new name, the Nationalist Party, which included a relatively-numerous group of dissidents from the Democrats. Other dissident groups were even weaker and less organized.

The *Seara Nova* group presented a coherent ideology aiming at a thorough reform of Portuguese mentality and politics. It was born as a reaction against the parties — as they were — and always claimed not to be a party but only a «group», willing to «help the parties to perfect themselves and to rule well». As such, *Seara Nova* posed as a defender of national interests. Its goals and programs combined a rather vague assertion of the usual Republican slogans with some other, more precise ideas: democratic socialism, non-Jacobin radicalism, internationalism and pacifism.

Integralismo Lusitano, on the rise since 1914, had a more original and more radical programme of future government and social organization, which opposed practically all the Republican ideologies. It opposed Liberalism (both political and economic) and almost all the basic principles of the French Revolution and other revolutions which stemmed from it.

The secret and semi-secret societies were very active, particularly in the period immediately before and after 1910. The *Carbonária* declined very quickly, and practically disappeared, giving way to several clubs or groupings which acted as private police bodies at the service of several parties and the institutions themselves. A clear line between political and criminal goals was often difficult to draw.

The role of the Freemasonry was very important. In 1914, there were some four thousand Portuguese masons. They played a part in the political, administrative, economic and social life of the country. More than half of the ministries in the First Republic were presided over by freemasons, and their time in government equated to more than 65 per cent of the period of the Democratic Republic.

The Republican constitution of 1911 emphasized the rights and warrants of the individual. In this, formulas adopted in the 19th century (such as the various freedoms, individual security, and property) were combined with proper Republican principles, such as social equality and laicism. It granted the right of resistance to any orders which might violate the individual guarantees. The constitution of 1911 also stressed the legislative power which, in fact, became the relevant one for most purposes. Parliament (officially named *Congress*) was made up of a Chamber of Deputies and a senate. Both chambers were directly elected by the people. The president of the Republic was elected by Congress every four years and could not be re-elected for the following term.

The Republican emphasis on democracy and popular representation enhanced the importance of the electoral body and underlined the importance of elections. Yet the concern in preparing a conscious body of citizens by means of education and in avoiding traditional influence by local authorities prevented a substantial enlargement of the number of voters and rejected immediate universal suffrage. In 1925, there were only 574 260 voters registered.

A general feature of Portuguese political life after 1910 was unquestionably the parliamentary, presidential and governmental instability. This situation had certainly begun before, during the monarchical period, and the Republic was simply its climax. The reasons for this were manifold. Undoubtedly, the excessive weight of parliament in the political life of the country accounted for much instability as well as party indiscipline, defective electoral laws, fake elections, political corruption and the like. Finally, one should not forget the manoeuvres of anti-Republicans, Catholics and foreigners (especially Spaniards), all aimed at subverting and discrediting the regime.

•

From 1911 to 1920, the population increased only very slightly, due to emigration, epidemics and World War I. Once the war was over and restrictions on free immigration had been imposed by many countries of the New World, the growth rate went up again, with the 1930 census registering 6 825 883 inhabitants. In the capital, the 435 thousand inhabitants in 1911 went up to almost 600 thousand in 1930.

Portugal's economic structure continued to be based mainly on agriculture. Wine, cork and fruit were the chief products and the chief exports, but the problem of wheat supply — particularly in Lisbon — absorbed much effort and concerned many governments in the period of 1910-26. World War I stimulated industrial activity, in Portugal as elsewhere in the world, particularly the production of canned fish (sardines). Other industries also developed, including cement, textiles and tobacco.

The main imports were wheat, textile fabrics, machinery, raw cotton, coal, codfish, sugar, steel and iron. The commercial balance showed a permanent deficit. English ships entering the Lisbon and Porto harbours also carried a heavy share of Portugal's external trade in 1924-25, more than one-fourth of the total tonnage was four to one over the Portuguese.

The Portuguese merchant navy showed some signs of prosperity, particularly after 1916, when the seizing of German and Austrian ships sheltered in Portuguese harbours suddenly increased the national tonnage. Of those ships, however, 42 were ceded to England and only half of them returned to Portugal. With them and the remaining 20, the government created the state-owned merchant navy (*Transportes Marítimos do Estado*), which operated for a few years.

Inherited from the monarchy, financial equilibrium was a primary problem in the country's political life. Though Afonso Costa managed to obtain a surplus, the outbreak of war posed the same problem once again. The situation only improved in 1923-24. Regarding currency, the Republic started by introducing thorough reforms in an attempt to put the new Portuguese unit (the *escudo*) on the same footing with other countries in Europe. When World War I began, problems with the new currency started and the value of the *escudo* dropped almost 20-fold. In 1924, premier Álvaro de Castro was able to stop its ruin.

A class of wealthy bourgeois, dependent upon banking activities, bulky trade and extensive landownership ruled Portugal as an oligarchy by 1910. They regarded the monarchy as a symbol of order and maintenance of their privileges and profits. They supported the Church and were supported by it. Their main enemy was not the world of workers and peasants, still insufficiently developed, but rather the urban middle-class. This class was deeply concerned with Portugal's backwardness and with the future of the colonies. It was greatly influenced by the French ideology, and it was anticlerical, republican and generally anti-socialist and patriotic.

In the larger towns, there was a small group of factory workers, mostly illiterate or poorly educated. Their class consciousness was minimal. Yet it was among them that a small nucleus of active socialists, anarchists (more numerous) and even communists was formed after 1918. Along with them, there were the lower strata of commercial and transport employees and civil servants.

The Provisional Government proclaimed the right to strike, albeit only after the workers had already embarked on an unprecedented strike movement, which went on until 1926. Other governments reorganized welfare, reduced or regulated working hours, provided social security and tried to build up houses for the workers. But social problems were not related only to the workers only. After 1919, the middle-class and the upper civil servants showed their dissatisfaction too. They complained about the fall in their real salaries, the small margin of profit in their businesses, the tax increase, the rise of labour unions and the labour movement, etc.

The new regime brought about a number of other interesting and highly-progressive laws. The acts of 1910-11 allowed divorce for all couples, made civil marriage compulsory for all marriages, granted equal rights to both sexes in marriage, and protected the legal rights of children. The first female university professor was appointed in 1911.

Despite the confiscation laws of 1820-34, the Portuguese Church persisted as a powerful force. Moreover, many religious orders had returned under various pretexts, namely the Jesuits. Once proclaimed, the Republic identified itself with the fight against the Church. All religious orders were expelled. An act of April 1911 (by Afonso Costa) separated Church and State, declared religion altogether free, forbade the teaching of Christianity in all schools, nationalized Church property, and strictly controlled every cult manifestation. The Separation Law of 1911 had been preceded by some other acts which clearly showed the anticlerical policy of the new regime. Thus, official religious oaths, including those taken in schools, were abolished; Catholic holidays were suppressed; and civil registry, i.e. compulsory recording of births, marriages and deaths by state officers, rather than by priests in the churches, was decreed for all. The religious question went on until the war. The bishops resisted the law, and were punished with provisional banishments from their bishoprics. The outbreak of World War I and Portugal's intervention after 1916 made a revival of the Church influence easier. In May 1917, the Church or some of its local elements possibly prepared — and certainly explored — the so-called Fátima apparitions, which soon had a great impact on the masses and caused an upsurge in devotion. The installation of a conservative and pro-clerical regime (December 1917) brought peace once more to the Portuguese Church. The trend now pointed to a compromise between Church and State.

The Republican reforms in primary education and the spirit behind them had an unquestionable impact on the quality of the education officially available to everyone. The new legislation established free, public education for all children — before and after reading age — and compulsory school attendance from age 7 to 10. Temporary or travelling schools were also established, particularly for teaching adults. Teacher salaries were increased. Yet the rate of illiteracy decreased only slightly: 69,7 per cent in 1911, 61,8 per cent in 1930.

Much more important were the reforms in technical and university education. The School of Industry and Commerce was split into two and raised to university level: the School of Engineering *(Instituto Superior Técnico)* and the School of Commerce *(Instituto Superior do Comércio),* both with new plans of studies and up-to-date discipline methods and equipment. The School of Agronomy and Veterinary Science was also divided into two: a School of Agronomy *(Instituto Superior de Agronomia)* and a School of Veterinary Science *(Escola de Medicina Veterinária)*. An act of 1918 reformed the lower technical schools and established a second university of commerce in Porto. All over the country, several new schools teaching agriculture, commerce and industry opened their doors year after year.

University education also received the attention of the Republican governments. As a basic principle, the Republic tried to put an end to Coimbra's centuries-long university monopoly and created new universities in Lisbon and Porto. Deep structural reforms affected all the colleges. A spelling reform was decreed. Afonso Costa created a new Ministry for Education. Besides the official education system, the Republican period witnessed a highly-interesting cultural boost, particularly in the fields of free learning and the popular spread of culture.

In the fields of science and technology, the Portuguese made some contribution to the world's progress in those days. Tropical sciences (medicine, botany, and zoology) remained among their main research areas. Ricardo Jorge's work on epidemics was decisive for understanding pestilent disease and its transmission. Research on cancer was promoted with the creation of a Cancer Institute, where some renowned doctors started working. Neurology, psychiatry, anatomy and physiology also included researchers of international renown.

However, the greatest scientific achievements in Portugal during the Republican era took place in aviation. After the war, the Portuguese attempted some wide-reaching air voyages:

Gago Coutinho and Sacadura Cabral flew an uncharted course from Lisbon to Madeira in March 1921, with no ships to guide them, and then again, in March-June 1922, they flew across the south Atlantic without guidance for the first time in a daring Lisbon-Rio de Janeiro trip. In that same year, aviators Brito Pais and Sarmento de Beires flew from Lisbon to Macao (China), and over the next six years several other air trips connected Portugal with her distant colonies.

The literary movement should be studied by an analysis of groups and currents rather than by focusing on individual authors. The first quarter of the 20th century did not include many great writers but contained many genres. The most valid Portuguese literature of the time was generally characterized by a nationalist tendency, as a reaction against the cosmopolitan realism of the late-1800s. In form and style, symbolism set the tone. Modern currents got underway by 1915, but had little impact on Portuguese society of the time. It is significant that Fernando Pessoa, the major Portuguese poet since Camões, was only «discovered» during and after World War II, most of his works being published posthumously.

In the arts, the persistence of old forms and styles was felt even more than in literature. Naturalism and nationalism prevailed in painting, sculpture and architecture, to general public approval. Music flourished in this period compared with the 19th century. National cinema also had an interesting phase of success and development. In the 1920s, a few high-quality movies were produced, and a short-lived national school of cinema was even opened.

THE «NEW STATE»

Cabeçadas's government, a compromise between the Republican public opinion and the right-oriented army groups, had no basis to endure. Backed by most of the Army, General Gomes da Costa staged a coup in June 1917 and imposed his full authority on a new cabinet. Yet his dubious reliability as a Rightist (he had belonged to the Radical Party) and his thorough ineptitude at political manoeuvring led to his quick downfall. On July 9, 1926, another Army coup, directed by monarchist General Sinel de Cordes, ousted Gomes da Costa (who was arrested and deported to the Azores) and replaced him with General Oscar Carmona, a Rightist man. Up until 1928, Sinel de Cordes and Carmona ruled Portugal in a typical military dictatorship. Cordes tried to reorganize finance and balance the budget, as well as stimulate Portugal's economy. But he had no preparation for such an undertaking and the results were disastrous. The deficit rose to unprecedented levels and the government had to ask the League of Nations for a loan.

The dictatorship was obviously backed by a large number of people, at least in the beginning. But, as the Rightist elements began to take the lead and the Fascist and Monarchist trends to assert themselves, more and more people regarded the new regime with concern, even within the armed forces. In February

1927, a violent revolution broke out in Porto and Lisbon, gathering together Army and Navy corps and thousands of civilians. It failed, with several hundreds dead or wounded. In 1928 and 1931, there were other uprisings, one of them in Madeira, Azores and Portuguese Guinea (led by deported politicians). Some abortive coups within the leading elements themselves also took place, but no essential changes occurred in the regime except that it became increasingly Right-oriented. The consequences of such uprisings and conspiracies were the development and improvement of the repressive machine. Thousands were arrested, many being deported to the overseas territories. Others fled the country and lived in exile.

Meanwhile, some dictatorial acts had changed the constitution, providing for a popular presidential election. Carmona was the only candidate and was therefore elected President of the Republic (April 1928). He entrusted Coronel Vicente de Freitas with the task of forming a new government. This cabinet included Professor Oliveira Salazar as its Finance Minister.

Oliveira Salazar, a 39-year-old professor of Economics at the University of Coimbra (School of Law), already had a political background by the time he accepted the Finance portfolio. Far from being unknown, he was regarded as a good deputy of the Right-wing, Catholic interests, and a sympathiser of the Monarchy. Moreover, his books and articles on economic and financial problems had made him praised and respected by friends and foes alike. In 1928, he accepted Vicente de Freitas's invitation on condition that he would control all the private budgets of the ministries and have the right of veto on every increase in expenditure. Gradually, Salazar's control of the government reached the political and military issues. Behind Salazar, of course, were powerful forces: capital and banking, which wanted free rein to expand without restrictions; the Church, proclaiming a new victory of the Cristian ideals and morals over the Republican demo-liberal and «masonic» atheism, and exploiting the Fátima «apparitions»; the majority of the Army; the Right-wing intellectuals; and most Monarchists.

In July 1932, President Carmona formally entrusted Salazar with forming a government of his own. It included a number of young civilians, mostly belonging to Salazar's own generation. Throughout 1932 and 1933, the final steps towards an authoritarian and corporate state took place. A new constitution was published in 1933, followed by other acts for the new corporate organization of the country. Late in 1934, the first general elections brought to the new Parliament an all-National Union representativeness (no other candidates could be nominated). In 1935, Carmona was re-elected President without opposition.

At home, Salazar's control of the regime increased as time went on. He became more and more of a dictator, more and more inclined to deify himself and to trust others less. The outbreak of World War II gave him some years of truce at home. Most of his enemies agreed to stop any subversive action until the end of the war. Portugal declared her neutrality from the very beginning, and was able to enforce it because of a complex group of motives.

Portugal's neutrality, however, had its price. Salazar had to tolerate the national humiliation of watching Portuguese Timor (in Indonesia) being invaded by Australia (1941), then by Japanese troops (1942), and fully occupied for three years. He was also compelled to allow the Allies (Great Britain and the United States) to establish military bases in the Azores (1943). With Franco, Salazar had signed a treaty of non-aggression and friendship as early as March 1939, which was later confirmed several times. The so-called «Iberian Bloc» thus came into existence. This new bulwark of Portugal's external policy counterbalanced the alliance with England.

To commemorate the eighth centenary of independence, and the third centenary of its restoration, the regime organized, in 1940, a full set of ceremonies, exhibitions, congresses and publications, of which the «Exposition of the Portuguese World» was the best example. Carefully prepared and brilliantly presented by some of the most competent architects, artists and decorators in Portugal, the Exposition was, in itself, a typical Fascist display in its manner of interpreting the past and abusing it to record the present and herald the future.

The Allied victory in Europe (May 1945) was a pretext for pro-democratic and pro-socialist demonstrations throughout the country. In September, the National Assembly was dissolved, and the government announced free elections for the coming November. Such an announcement aroused great agitation, both within and outside the regime. Tens of thousands gave their adherence to the newly created MUD *(Movimento de Unidade Democrática* or Movement of Democratic Unity), a sort of Popular Front against the «New State». The opposition soon realized, however, that the freedom granted was very relative, and that it had no time to promote a political organization of its own which could fight the regime at the polis. All of the National Union nominees were therefore elected without question. Shortly afterward, a vast purge aiming at those who had subscribed to the MUD jailed several hundreds, dismissed many civil servants (including army and navy officials), and placed under surveillance a large number of people. The entire repressive machine was improved.

From 1945 on, the existence of an opposition could not be denied. It expressed itself in many different ways, as a permanent affront to the government. In the presidential elections of 1949 (Carmona had been re-elected again in 1942 without opposition), the MUD nominated aged general Norton de Matos, who campaigned vigorously with the help of a remarkable group of advisers. He denounced all the failures and contradictions of Salazarism, and announced his intentions of restoring democracy to the country. However, no guarantees of free elections were given, and when the MUD candidate realized that the situation was unchanged, he withdrew from the race and Carmona was therefore re-elected once again. When Carmona died, in April 1951, elections presented little danger to the government. Salazar's candidate, general Craveiro Lopes, was elected without opposition.

Fearing a communist takeover and not wanting to take any risks, the Western Allies were now definitely backing Salazar. Portugal became a member of NATO from its very beginning (1949) and posed as a defender of the «free» world. To appease international public opinion and rising criticism of colonialism, an amendment to the constitution repealed the Colonial Act of 1930 and introduced some changes in the status of the «natives», as well as in the official names of the colonies (from then on called «overseas provinces»). The Soviet Union allowed Portugal to enter the United Nations, along with several other countries, in 1955.

The presidential elections of 1958 showed unmistakable dissensions within the regime. President Craveiro Lopes was not renominated by the National Union. Instead, admiral Américo Tomás, Minister of the Navy since 1944 and a docile admirer of the premier's, was chosen. The opposition chose air force general Humberto Delgado, an acting civil servant.

Delgado proved to be the right man for the situation. He easily established close contact with the people and aroused widespread enthusiasm throughout Portugal. As in 1949, the regime feared for its survival and prepared military action in case of a possible takeover by the opposition. Although no guarantees of electoral freedom were granted, and no poll control by the opposition was accepted, Delgado decided to fight to the end. Official figures gave him a quarter of the votes, but he always claimed to be the real winner.

Once the election was over, repression was intensified again. General Delgado was dismissed from his position, then forced to ask for political asylum at the Brazilian Embassy. The bishop of Porto, who wrote a letter to Salazar insisting on a change of government methods and policies, had to leave the country too.

Political turmoil continued. In January 1961, the general situation worsened with the capture of the liner Santa Maria by political exiles, in connection with the Angolan uprising in February. In April of the same year, the Minister of Defence, general Botelho Moniz, attempted a coup against Salazar, but failed. In December, the Portuguese possessions in India were invaded and lost, an event that very much shook the regime's prestige. All this led to a new military uprising, on January 1, 1962, in Beja (Alentejo), where the Under-Secretary of the Army lost his life. Finally, a widespread student movement broke out in March (mostly in Lisbon), and lasted through to May. It included strikes, demonstrations, protests and mass arrests.

Yet it was still possible for Salazar to emerge victorious from this crisis and start another period of stabilization (albeit short, and the last one). Utterly divided, the opposition ceased to pose any great threat to the regime. In 1965, admiral Américo Tomás was re-elected President. The main question had now shifted from Portugal to the overseas provinces, where African revolts, acts of terrorism and foreign participation were a concern to everyone.

By the late-1960s, and despite the apparent maintenance of order and calm, the regime was no longer what it had been. Division plagued its ranks; Salazar's obvious senility and inflexibility endangered administration and general policy. Control had almost completely been transferred onto the censorship services and the Secret Police. Repression haunted the late-1960s as it had in the days of triumphant Fascism. To many people, it became clear that something had to change soon.

The change came in a most unexpected way. Early in September 1968, a chair collapsed under Salazar, whose head hit the ground. The result was a blood clot in his brain. Following an operation to remove it, the premier suffered a brain haemorrhage and his condition was soon considered hopeless for purposes of practical recovery. On September 27, president Américo Tomás had to replace the 79-year-old head of the government and appoint Marcelo Caetano instead.

Marcelo Caetano's policy proved to be rather cautious. Aware of the difficult situation he inherited, he tried, in a general way, to keep things as they were, with nothing but slight and almost imperceptible modifications. He allowed the return of hundreds or even thousands of exiles, including known communists and the Bishop of Porto, who had been forced to depart in 1958; he restricted the unbridled power of the State Police and censorship activity was restrained; members of the opposition could meet in a so-called historical Republican Congress in Aveiro. Some «subversive» works began to appear in bookstores. Theatre and cinema, as far as plays and film exhibitions (with either social or «immoral» contents) were concerned, gained more freedom. In public places, people could speak more freely and fearlessly. At the National Assembly elected in 1969, one fifth to one fourth of representatives — the so-called liberal wing — showed some tendencies against the regime's immobilism. The National Union *(União Nacional)* itself changed its name to Popular National Action *(Acção Nacional Popular)*. However, Marcelo Caetano kept the structure of the «New State» in its essence. Portuguese troops continued to be sent to Africa in order to fight the rebels. No political parties were allowed and no amnesty was granted. Freedom of association was denied. The foreign policy did not suffer any changes at all. The corporative system was kept intact. No new laws for the press ever appeared.

By the end of 1969, the «honeymoon» between Marcelo Caetano and the opposition reached its term. In the spring of 1970, Mário Soares, one of the opposition leaders, who had already been deported during Salazar's days, had to leave again to exile to avoid arrest. Other opposition leaders were persecuted or imprisoned. The university students' hostility towards the regime, as well as the demands for a reformed educational system, prevented the school terms to go on normally. The military situation overseas was almost stationary, but the cost of a permanent guerrilla war increased and impended on all aspects of national life. The army was unable to win a guerrilla fight which could last indefinitely. Ten years of hostilities without a predictable outcome, and the absence of any kind of dialogue with the enemy frustrated and tired the military involved. The number of desertions increased along with the number of injured and dead.

Politically, the «New State» showed itself incapable of renovation, due to the rigidity and archaic nature of its structures, and also to the weight of a group of «historicals» led by the president of the Republic himself, Américo Tomás. Marcelo Caetano maintained all the repressive machine of Salazar's time. The general elections of 1973 were not much different from those of Salazar's time. The «liberal wing» disappeared.

The world crisis, combined with the consequences of the colonial war, cast a shadow over the entire country. Inflation began to frighten many people. On the other hand, tension increased between the upper-bourgeoisie, which controlled and benefited the most from the war and the capitalist rise, and a medium and small bourgeoisie in economic and demographic expansion, anxious to achieve a certain status within the state machine, as well as a share in the profits. As most of the urban proletarians were becoming a part of the bourgeois ranks, the proletariat itself was a major participant in this social conflict.

In 1973, the governor of Guinea, general António de Spínola (a prestigious figure as a military man and as a defender of a new policy of native participation) spoke out against the political and military monoletheism. He was replaced in his government. Around the same time, a vast conspiracy was held among a group of Army captains based on a minor question about promotions and careers, but that soon turned into a general plot against the regime. In February 1974, general Spínola, with the approval of Costa Gomes (Head of the Armed Forces Staff) published a famous book, *Portugal e o Futuro* (*Portugal and the Future*), where he openly criticized both the internal and the external Portuguese policies. He defended a federalist solution for the overseas provinces. Quite subtly, he also defended a coup against the government.

From then on, events unfolded quickly. On March 14, Spínola and Costa Gomes were dismissed from their functions. On the 16th, a first military revolt took place in Caldas da Rainha. It was rapidly quashed, for it lacked organization and coordination. One month later, on April 25th 1974, another military movement, this time with the active participation of most units and much quicker and precise, put an end to the regime. There was no bloodshed nor any significant resistance. The government surrendered in Lisbon and Marcelo Caetano and Américo Tomás, along with other ministers, were arrested and deported to Madeira and, later, to Brazil. A National Salvation Junta was formed under the presidency of Spínola, with Costa Gomes as the second figure. The «New State» had come to an end.

•

The Portuguese authoritarian state had as roots the so-called Integralismo Lusitano, the Catholic fighting groups, such as the CADC (*Centro Académico de Democracia Cristã*) and the Catholic Centre (*Centro Católico*); and other Right-wing political groups within the parliamentary Republic. Italian Fascism and General Primo de Rivera's authoritarian regime in Spain and, later, the Austrian and German authoritarian regimes also had their influences on building up the Portuguese system.

Yet, it would be hard to call the army rebellion of 1926 a Fascist movement. Action had been taken against the «corruption» and «degradation» of the parliamentary republic rather than against the parliamentary institutions as such. The «programme» of the Revolution encompassed a long series of vague aspirations which everybody in the country wished to realize: inquiry into the public services, suspicious civil servants, and the «great fortunes»; economies and good administration; valorisation of the *escudo* and decrease in the cost of living; road repair; an end to nationalization and return to private companies of the nationalized services; reforms of the army and the navy; increase in the number of schools; reforms in justice; better administration of the colonies; etc.

The military dictatorship of 1926-28 carefully avoided any action that might be interpreted as aiming at a restoration of the monarchy. In 1932, former King Manuel's death inflicted a blow to any monarchical hopes. With his death, all serious chances of a monarchical restoration died too. Most Monarchists, including Salazar himself, realized this, and supported the Republic. A good many Integralists, waiting for a more favourable time, were not hostile to the Republican institutions. These two facts helped maintain and strengthen the *status quo,* even against violent opposition from the organized Republican groups.

By 1928, the first steps in shaping a new order were being taken, but rather slowly. In the fall of 1929, Salazar described the future constitutional reorganization as one based upon a «solid, prudent and conciliatory nationalism»; emphasized the roles of the family, the moral and economic corporation, the parish and the municipality; and uttered the slogan which would become famous: «Nothing against the Nation, all for the Nation.» In 1931, he defined the future situation as the setting up of a «well understood political, economic and social nationalism, controlled by the unquestionable sovereignty of the strong State». Yet Salazar always spoke against totalitarian regimes and criticised both the Italian Fascist and the German Nazi systems. He clearly distinguished between authoritarianism and totalitarianism.

The New State should be social and corporate. Its fundamental cell should be the family, its basic elements the moral and economic corporations, where the interests of both employers and employees would, together, aim at the common «national» interests. Therefore, the following were created: the national unions, composed of employees; the *grémios*, gathering together individual employers; and the *casas dos pescadores*, associations of fishermen and their employers. The «corporations» proper would constitute, according to the law that created them, «the unitary organization of the production forces, completely representing their interests». Besides the economic ones, there would also be the *moral corporations*, for public assistance and charity, and the *cultural corporations*, aiming at scientific, literary, artistic and similar goals. Thus, the corporative state tried to shape a new Portugal. It built up an economically organized country, an interventionist state essentially different from the liberal, «laissez-faire» Republican order.

In his key speeches of 1939, Salazar clearly put aside the concepts of individual freedom and party organisation. The party must be replaced by the association. Therefore, all political parties and secret societies were disbanded when the new constitution was put into effect in 1933, and only a «union of all Portuguese», typically christened as «National Union» (*União Nacional*) was tolerated. After 1936, the regime's militia, the *Legião Portuguesa* (Portuguese Legion) and the *Mocidade Portuguesa* (Portuguese Youth) were created. Both organisations stuck to the typical Fascist uniforms (green shirts), the Roman salute, the terminology, the internal structure, certain slogans, and so on.

The other authoritarian institutions of the New State were the repressive mechanisms. Censorship of periodicals was instituted shortly after the revolution of May 1926, and maintained ever since. It was gradually extended to other media such as theatre, cinema, radio and television. It maintained a check not only on political or military matters, but also on morals, patterns of behaviour, religion and every news item or address susceptible of influencing the people in a «dangerous» way. The political police were first called PVDE (*Polícia de Vigilância e Defesa do Estado*), then had its name changed to PIDE (*Polícia Internacional e de Defesa do Estado*). As with the Inquisition, the Portuguese Secret Police reaches such extremes of power and pervasiveness that it defied the authority of the state itself —

including that of the Armed Forces — and gradually became a state within the state. And like the Inquisition, it had to justify its own existence and power by often «inventing» non-existent threats to the regime's security and «making up» communists and other opponents to the New State out of tenuous presumptions or hearsay. The insistence of the Secret Police on the most sophisticated forms of torture, as well as other physical and psychological pressures, their use of dismal civilian prisons and concentration camps (a major one was in operation in the Cape Verde islands, its name, Tarrafal, becoming a symbol of the New State methods of terror); their breaking into residences and seizure of personal belongings; their presence everywhere, all this cemented Salazar's power over the decades and helped explain the famous «order in the streets» he was so proud of claiming.

Other, less evident forces were often more relevant in achieving the goals of the regime than the obvious censorship and police authority. This was true of the political pressures on civil servants, which lead to a complete taming of most elements, including instructors and army and navy forces. Pressure was also applied to firms to dismiss or deny admission to politically-unreliable people.

The constitutional text (1933) reflected a clear compromise between the «demo-liberal» principles and the Integralist-Fascist tendencies. The Constitution defined the State as unitary and corporative. It classified power in four branches: the President of the Republic, the National Assembly, the government, and the tribunals. It gave the President extensive powers, comparable to those which the Constitutional Charter granted the king; moreover, it provided for the President to be elected by popular vote. A presidential regime might have resulted, yet Salazar's thirty-six-year-old premiership transferred power to the government and reduced the President to almost nothing.

The National Assembly *(Assembleia Nacional)* was formed by representatives elected by the people for a four-year term. Its functions were to supervise administration, and to vote the acts proposed by the government or the representatives. In practice, the latter rarely happened, most laws coming from the government, and the role of the National Assembly has always been minimal. A Corporative Chamber composed of representatives of the corporations, the municipalities, the Church, the universities, the institutes of charity, and the bodies of administration assisted the National Assembly and the government in law-making. The government became the real source of power, and its head (President of the Council of Ministers) the true and sole leader of the country.

Several amendments changed the Constitution now and then but generally on secondary points. The only major change took place in 1959, by making the election of the President dependent upon an electoral college.

The size of the electorate did not significantly increase in forty years, although college-graduated women and female heads of family were only given voting rights in the early 1930s. A considerable part of the people qualified to vote never did register, while a good many others were written off the balloting rolls. As a rule, a high level of abstentions featured the electoral «farces» (as oppositionists called them), although the official figures almost always gave over 80 or 90 per cent victory results.

The Catholic feature of the New State must be emphasised but not exaggerated, for Salazar's regime never posed as an «apostolic» system engaged in some kind of crusade against anti-Catholic elements. No attempt was made to reunite Church and State. No one was ever persecuted or even discriminated against because of their religious faith or atheist principles.

And the Concordat of 1940, while yielding to some Catholic requirements such as the abolition of divorce for couples married in church or the teaching of religion in schools, neither put an end to civil marriage and civil divorce nor gave back to the Church all the property confiscated since 1910. Cemeteries were not sacralised. Religious orders were only accepted providing they engaged in some kind of charitable or educational work. Religious oaths were not re-established. Classes on religion were not compulsory and no exams were required. Official schools of theology could never be re-established at the universities.

More than any definite clerical attitude, Salazar rather emphasized his stance in defence of «Christian and Western civilization» and the creating of a state well equipped for that purpose. He often posed as a prophet of the world's tragedies because of the Western leader's relinquishment of the true values of Western civilization, which he always underlined, and because of their surrender to the forces of «evil». Such forces were, of course, embodied by communism.

•

When Salazar took to power, in 1928, Portugal was obsessed with the financial crisis. Salazar's first budget, that of 1928-29, accomplished a miracle. From 1928-29, all Portuguese budgets were balanced.

This had become a sort of spell by the New State and a corner stone of its administration, a symbol of good management and continuous progress.

World War II brought some prosperity to the country. Being neutral, Portugal could sell her products quite favourably without greatly disturbing expenditures for war material. By 1946, revenues had nearly doubled while currency debasement did not go beyond ten per cent. Gold reserves reached high levels, creating monetary stability. This trend continued after the war.

Comparable in so many ways to mid-19th-century Fontism, the New State embarked on an extensive program of public works. This policy aimed at a development and betterment of infrastructures considered instrumental in the shaping of the country's new economy. Road building was accompanied by bridge building, several outstanding and spectacular bridges being erected (the arch-bridge over the Douro at Porto, opened in 1963; the bridge over the Tagus in Lisbon, the longest suspension bridge in Europe, opened in 1966). Telegraph and telephone networks expanded remarkably too, and port facilities were considerably improved. A policy of land irrigation and electrification led to building of numerous dams scattered all over the country. Yet Portugal was far from having electricity everywhere in the 1960s. Public works encompassed many other aspects of life such as housing (houses for workers), health (hospitals), sports (stadia), justice (courthouses and prisons), administration (government buildings), army and navy (barracks, shipyards), tourism and culture (state-owned inns and restoration of monuments), etc.

The public works policy bore fruit, enabling the rapid economic development of Portugal in the 1950s and the 1960s. In the balance of trade, for instance, exports rose twenty-eight times between 1926 and 1967. As imports increased only twelve times, the usual deficit of the balance of trade declined in relation to the trade volume. Altogether, the role of industry in exports rose from one-third (1926) to almost two-thirds by the late-1960s. Imports hardly changed in character. Portugal continued to order all kinds of manufactured items, oil, coal, and other industrial raw-materials, as well as grain.

Despite the great changes and accomplishments which took place in most economic fields, particularly after World War II, the New State could not transform Portugal into a well-developed country. The main reason was that in other underdeveloped countries of Europe the rate of economic growth was much faster than in Portugal, and was coupled with a wise policy of cultural development which Portugal lacked. The number of emigrants leaving the country in search of better salaries was a clear proof of poor conditions at home. The war in Africa, if it provided a stimulus for economic development and migration to Angola and Mozambique, also hampered prospects of a faster growth rate at home, with 50 per cent of the national budget being applied to military expenses. In the field of agriculture, one of the main concerns for many years was to achieve self-sufficiency in grain production. Much more successful and useful was the tree-planting policy, which converted barren fields and mountain soil into green and productive lands. Among the traditional cultures, vineyards somewhat expanded to the 1940s. Olive oil, cork and fruit had their production substantially enlarged too. Fishing also developed, with important results for the canning industry.

From 1930 to 1968, the population of Portugal increased more than one-third. The growth rate was particularly high from 1930 to 1940. Figures, as shown by decennial censuses, were 6 825 883 in 1930, and 8 889 392 in 1960. But the growing emigration brought this figure down to 8 668 267 in 1970. Urban growth continued, the Lisbon and Porto areas attracting a great influx from the rural and the more backward hinterland. In 1960, 25,1 per cent of all Portuguese lived in those two areas.

A policy of mass education was never a top priority for the New State, despite periodical claims to the contrary by officials. The total rate of illiteracy went down slowly until the

1950s. Compulsory school years increased from three to four in 1960 and then to six in 1967.

Secondary and technical education received comparatively more attention from the government. New high schools and technical schools rose everywhere and school population increased. Portuguese secondary education did retain quality, despite the heavy political indoctrination in subjects like history, philosophy, and «political and administrative organization of the nation». The highly centralized education system led to the so-called «single books», officially approved by the government and imposed on all schools as the only authorized textbooks.

Higher education generally declined, a result of political harassment and mistrust of instructors and students alike. Periodic purges deprived the universities of some of their best talent, while political reasons prevented recruiting qualified staff, hindered promotions and pushed up mediocre but politically-reliable people. In 1930, a government act created a Technical University in Lisbon encompassing some existing schools. It was only after the 1950s that the university system progressed a little, benefiting from the country's economic expansion and the enrolment of larger and larger numbers of young people. In the fields of medicine and engineering, however, some real progress was achieved, with the creation of several excellent laboratories and other centres of research, and the development of the existing ones.

Competition with the all-pervasive government control of education started only in the 1950s, with the establishment of the wealthy Gulbenkian Foundation and several other less important private groups with cultural and scientific purposes. The Church also managed to create a Catholic University, and several private schools for less formal and more practical matters (business management, foreign languages, hotel management, tourism, etc.) opened their doors to more and more students.

Outside regular education, the general development of culture was jeopardized by a growing interference of the government and its mistrust of progressive currents of thought. In the world of letters, censorship operated again and again, erasing or mutilating articles, bringing periodicals to an abrupt end and preventing others from appearing. Major prose and poetry writers of the time were Aquilino Ribeiro and Miguel Torga, both Nobel prize candidates; Ferreira de Castro, most of whose works were translated into numerous languages; José Régio; Alves Redol, the greatest exponent of neo-realism; and António Sérgio, a philosopher and essayist. One of the great moments in modern Portuguese cultural life was undoubtedly the posthumous «discovery» of Fernando Pessoa's work. His major books were all published in the 1940s and 1950s.

Political ideologies had lesser impact on the arts, yet the trend toward centralization in every field did influence the development of architecture, sculpture, painting and other arts. The foundation of the National Secretariat of Propaganda — later called National Secretariat for Information — in 1933 was instrumental in creating a fascist «national» style, which pervaded the arts at least until the 1950s. Under the direction of António Ferro, the SNP-SNI undertook multiple efforts in every artistic field, most perhaps with typical political goals, but some others with highly-interesting features of art development.

Science and technology developed unevenly. In some fields, such as medicine, Portugal's contribution was a major one. Professor Egas Moniz (1874-1955) received the Nobel prize in 1949 for his discoveries in brain angiography and leucotomy.

He founded an important school of research in those and other fields. Tropical medicine, too, had a remarkable development in Portugal. Many sciences however, stagnated or declined, for lack of funding devoted to equipment and research, or because of political discrimination.

THE OVERSEAS EMPIRE IN THE 20TH CENTURY

The Republican administration decided to carry on decentralization on a wide basis. The so-called Organic Laws set up the basis for financial and administrative decentralization. They also established basic principles on how to deal with indigenous populations. In each colony, natives were to be tutored and protected by the governor and his subordinates under special legislation. Private law would follow their usages and traditions. No political rights were acknowledged to them except within their own tribal life.

According to the laws of August 1920, the Portuguese colonies would have financial autonomy and a greater degree of decentralization. Functions of administration would belong to the governor of each colony, assisted by an executive council and supervised by the Portuguese Executive. When the latter thought it convenient, executive powers could be temporarily delegated to High Commissioners, whose functions would be merged with those of governor. The government appointed former cabinet ministers Norton de Matos and Brito Camacho as the first High Commissioners to Angola and Mozambique.

The policy of colonial autonomy came to an end with the gradual definition of the New State. The trend towards decentralization was reversed, and a more centralized system, similar to the one prior to 1914, restored. Successive laws enhancing control by Lisbon Governors-general replaced High Commissioners again. A new expression, «Portuguese Colonial Empire», made its appearance in the official terminology.

The «Colonial Act» of 1930 enforced the basic principles of 1926. Conceived as a sort of Constitution for the overseas territories, later appended to the Constitution of 1933, it introduced some ultra-nationalist tendencies. Thus it declared to belong «to the organic essence of the Portuguese Nation the historical mission of possessing and colonizing overseas dominions, as well as civilizing the native populations encompassed by them». Another article gave the state the right to compel natives to work under certain circumstances. Article 22 spoke of «special statutes» for the natives, according to their stage of evolution. The principles of the «New State» concerning colonial administration were also embodied in the «Organic Charter of the Colonial Empire» and the Overseas Administrative Reform, both enacted in 1933.

President Carmona paid his first visit to São Tomé and Angola (1938), then to Cape Verde and Mozambique (1939). His successors, Craveiro Lopes and Américo Tomás, visited all the overseas territories again and again. Other frequent visitors were the colonial ministers.

All the legislation concerning natives aimed at bringing the «non-civilized» Africans and Timorese up into European civilization and the Portuguese nation, by means of a gradual change in their usages and their moral and social values. Local cultures, social organization and law should be respected and maintained, but only on a transitional basis.

After the end of World War II, anticolonialism gained a new dimension. Critics of the Portuguese colonial system arose, denouncing the serfdom of most Africans and the economic stagnation of the colonies. To appease this first wave of attacks, the Constitution was amended. The words «colony» and «colonial» disappeared altogether, giving way to «overseas province» and «overseas». The official designation of «empire» faded away. The condition of «natives» was officially defined as transitory. A new «Organic Law» appeared in 1953, followed by a more enlightened «Statute of the Portuguese Natives of the Provinces of Guinea, Angola, and Mozambique» (1954). In this way, the Portuguese government could evade the United Nations Charter with all its clauses on the responsibility and duties of colonial countries regarding dependent territories. In 1961, all the inhabitants of Angola, Mozambique and Guinea officially became full Portuguese citizens.

The Republican ethics proclaimed liberty and equality for all, and denounced all kinds of abuses practiced both at home and in the overseas provinces. No wonder that, once victorious, the Republicans tried very hard to correct every fault in colonial administration and to introduce a new spirit of governing. Governor Norton de Matos, twice governor of Angola, was the best-known exponent of the Republican «new-look» towards Africans. He curbed, as much as he could, the compulsory recruitment of African labour. The labour code was suspended during his governorship. He forbade corporal punishment, published an abundant set of decrees providing official protection to the African, curbed alcoholism, and instituted committees for assistance to the natives. He also tried, and often succeeded, in repatriating Angolan workers living in São Tomé. At the same time, a plan to convert many Africans into permanent farmers was drafted and partly executed.

The 1930s and the 1940s were regressive and stagnant periods in regard to protection of Africans. The Republican programme required a permanent struggle against tradition, prejudice and vested interests. With the change of policies in Lisbon, in 1926, the white settlers were given much more freedom than before. The fight against capitalist interests and their consequent exploitation of native labour slowed down. Disguised forms of slavery reappeared. Although labour conditions improved considerably, exploitation of Africans went on, because of economic needs and long-established traditions.

What must be emphasized is that economic motivations, rather than racial attitudes, were generally behind the Portuguese-African relationships. Only in Mozambique, and by no means consistently, was there some racist bias against the blacks, through Rhodesian or South African influence.

•

By 1910, Portuguese authority was more or less respected by the native populations of Angola, Mozambique, Guinea and Timor. The Republican administration, placing its emphasis on the civilian rather than the military aspect, tried to avoid as much as possible «subjugation» campaigns in the traditional manner. Yet military campaigns did occur in north Mozambique, in West Timor, in northwest Angola, and especially in Guinea. World War I fostered some rebellions against the Portuguese by German influence, both in Angola and in Mozambique. Germans raided the border of the two colonies as early as 1914, inflicting some casualties on the local garrisons. Lisbon sent two expeditions to Angola (1914-15) and four to Mozambique (1914-17). In Angola, the fight with the Germans did not last long and was limited to border skirmishes, marches and counter-marches. In Mozambique, war brought about worse results.

After a brief period of success when the Portuguese troops reoccupied Kionga and invaded Tanganyika, German counteroffensives under Von Lettow-Vorbeck pushed the Portuguese south nearly to Quelimane (summer of 1918).

A few native uprisings and strikes still happened here and there in the 1920s, but with minor participation of tribes and still less impact on the colonies' general life. In the 1930s Guinea registered some agitation too. Police operations were enough to put them down. World War II was only directly felt in Timor.

Although independence movements in Portuguese Africa began only in the 1960s, their roots can be traced back to the time of the first Republic. Unrestricted freedom of press and association encouraged several groups of Europeanized blacks and mixed-race people living both in the colonies and in Portugal proper, to form societies and start newspapers where they denounced the abuses of the administration. But by the early 1930s, authoritarian repression spreading from Portugal to the overseas muzzled open protests and confined the African societies and newspapers to more harmless activities.

After World War II, the general awakening of Africa and the widespread independence movements had their impact on the Portuguese colonies too. In February 1961, some hundreds of members of the MPLA (*Movimento Popular de Libertação de Angola*) attacked several prisons, barracks and the broadcasting station of Luanda. The government, however, was aware of the potential rebellion and had sent troops to Angola beforehand. It could thus control the situation and deter the attackers. A widespread feeling of fear among the settlers led to the slaughtering of scores of blacks and the flight of hundreds of others, many of whom joined the insurgents. In March, tribes in northern Angola rebelled with Congolese backing and massacred several hundred settlers. All this brought about increasing repression from the side of authorities and whites alike, with the support of many natives as well. A guerrilla war started in northern Angola, with some territory actually occupied throughout the years.

The government tried to solve the problem with military action. Relatively well-trained and well-equipped troops were sent in larger and larger numbers. The PIDE displayed no less activity, their agents in Africa outnumbering those active in Portugal. The administration realized, however, that other means were necessary. Government funds poured in as never before. Attention was finally paid to long-lasting claims. Africans were granted full rights, better jobs, and higher salaries. Public education and welfare were improved. Public works were intensified.

Nonetheless, guerrilla warfare did not fade away. On the contrary, it increased with the outbreak of rebellions in Guinea (1963) and north Mozambique (1964). In Guinea, the PAIGC (*Partido Africano da Independência da Guiné e Cabo Verde*) controlled one-third to one-half of the colony (but no cities) by the late-1960s. In Mozambique, African unity was achieved with FRELIMO (*Frente de Libertação de Moçambique*), which developed its activity in the north. The Angolan guerrilla had several phases and was supported by several revolutionary movements, each one acting on its own. Yet, the Portuguese military effort prevented any significant conquest of territory. By 1974, Portugal was far from losing control of the situation. In Mozambique, revolutionary unity made the war more difficult for the Portuguese. However, the situation there was not particularly difficult in 1974. More important were probably the quarrels between the white settlers and the military, accused of neglecting their protection.

Thus, the independence of both colonies, in 1975, depended more on the political consequences of the revolution at home than on a military defeat on the African territories.

The smaller colonies were not free from agitation. In São Tomé, an uprising of African workers, because of labour conditions, led to violent repression but also to some attempts at meeting the demands of labour. On the Gulf of Guinea, armed forces of the newly-created republic of Dahomey ousted the few Portuguese officials from the fortress of Ajudá. In India, Nehru's administration vainly tried for years to induce a voluntary withdrawal of the Portuguese from Goa, Damão and Diu. In 1954, two enclaves near Damão were permanently occupied by India. In December 1961, Indian troops invaded Goa, Damão and Diu. Greatly outnumbered, the Portuguese offered symbolic resistance only.

•

The democratic analysis shows a growth in the white populations both in Angola and Mozambique. In Angola the number of white settlers increased from less than 10 thousand in 1910 to about 50 thousand in 1930. By the end of the 1960s, there were more than 300 thousand whites in Angola. In Mozambique, white population jumped from little more than 5 thousand to nearly 50 thousand in 1950, but it doubled in 1960 and doubled again at the end of the decade. Luanda and Lourenço Marques contained at least half of the Europeanized population. Lourenço Marques being located too far south, there was a quick development of other towns scattered all over the country: Beira, the second city of the colony, Quelimane, João Belo, Tete, Vila Cabral and Port Amélia. In Angola, Lobito rose from nothing in 1910 to becoming the second most important town, in 1960. It was followed by Nova Lisboa (formerly Huambo), practically founded by Norton de Matos in 1912 and later officially named capital of Angola. In the smaller colonies, with the exception of Macao, no large towns rose in any of the territories.

The economic development of all the Portuguese overseas provinces, but particularly Angola and Mozambique, was irregular and uneven. The colonies depended upon foreign markets and foreign capital more than Portugal's.

Until the first years of the 20th century, rubber was the chief product exported by Angola and the main source of its revenue. From 1911 on, rubber fell sharply and Angola faced a difficult period of adjustment until World War I. In the 1920s, both coffee and cotton were on their way up. After 1921, diamonds started providing Angola with a new source of wealth. In the 1930s, coffee had become number one in the colony's exports, followed by diamonds, fish meal, maize, cotton and sisal. In the 1950s, iron ore was discovered and quickly ranked among Angola's sources of income. So did oil, actively explored in the 1960s. Foreign investments were encouraged by the Republic, and extensive economic concessions were granted to a few powerful companies. The *Diamang* (Angola Diamond Company), founded in 1917, saw its concessions further enlarged and confirmed. It became a true state within Angola.

The economic development of Mozambique followed a different pattern. More than half of the colony belonged to three private companies, two of which (the Mozambique Company and the Nyasa Company) were chartered. Altogether, Mozambique's main production and sources of wealth did not change much in fifty years. As in Angola, rubber played a major role at the beginning of the century, but not so exclusively as on the West Coast. Oleaginous products (copra, sesame, peanuts) held first place. Sugar came third. When rubber declined and finally disappeared, sugar held second place, followed by sisal and cotton. Tea also became a major source of wealth.

The Mozambique Company prospered and contributed to the colony's development until 1923. The Beira railroad and the

Beira port permitted ever-increasing international traffic. The Company proportionally opened more schools and could register a higher attendance than the government-administered sector. It built new railroads, opened a substantial road network, and made several other improvements.

The Republican decentralization system and the High Commissioner regime failed to foster Mozambique's development as it did Angola's. Mozambique possessed a tighter and more developed capitalist structure, much more dependent on British capitals. Yet, the Republican period meant for Mozambique a considerable development of infrastructures, namely port equipment and railroads. Lourenço Marques and Beira, due to their international importance, were equipped with modern facilities and therefore attracted most of Transvaal's and Rhodesia's traffic.

Industrial development in both colonies was paid, comparatively, much less attention. Until the 1960s, Portugal followed a typical colonial policy of fostering the production of raw materials but discouraging industrial activities in the overseas provinces. The outbreak of the guerrilla war changed the whole picture and brought about a quick industrial rise.

Subsistence in the smaller colonies, Macao and São Tomé excepted, was not an easy one. Their economies and financial situation were far from brilliant, despite the fact that they frequently displayed surpluses in the balance of trade and the budget.

Well aware of the importance of Catholic missions to Europeanize Africans, the Republic did not impose on the overseas the anticlerical policy followed at home. Few missionaries belonging to orders ever left because of the Republican legislation. Persecutions were few and did not last. On the other hand, the lay missions created after 1910 had little time to develop and prosper, not withstanding the subsidies which the law granted them. The new Organic Statute of the Portuguese Catholic Missions (1926) enforced the nationalist spirit so dear to the «new order». It repressed foreign and non-Catholic missions, increased subsidies, and openly favoured the Catholic priests. The Church was given a free hand to operate in all Portuguese colonies under a highly-privileged situation. The Concordat of 1940 and the Missionary Agreement of the same year, both signed with the Vatican, further enhanced the possibilities of the Church in Christianising and civilizing the natives.

An important result of the agreements between Church and state after 1940 was the thorough reorganization of the ecclesiastical structure in the Portuguese empire. Angola and Mozambique were raised to archbishoprics, two other dioceses being created in Angola, and two in Mozambique. Guinea was also separated from Cape Verde and turned into an apostolic prefecture. In Timor, another diocese came into existence. In this way, ecclesiastical organization did coincide with the political shape of the Portuguese empire. Later development of both Angola and Mozambique led to new dioceses. In Asia, the decline of the Portuguese influence put an end to the right of patronage.

Cultural development lagged very much behind the economic one. For many years, only Cape Verde, Macao and Portuguese India had some educational framework worth mentioning. Emigration increase and the Republican policy of fostering education brought about the need for more primary schools and the beginnings of a somewhat higher education.

The great leap forward happened in the 1950s and the 1960s in all the overseas provinces, but especially in Angola and Mozambique. Educational reforms created a unified governmental system for Africans, all mission schools being officialised and offering the same kind of education everywhere. Secondary education showed a smaller, yet important, increase. The need to respond to autonomist tendencies led the government to create universities in both colonies (1963), which developed rapidly.

In the other territories, growth was less spectacular yet thoroughly positive. By the early 1970s the educational system in the Portuguese overseas provinces, although far from being the best in Africa, showed an undeniable capacity for quick growth and could compare favourably with many others on that continent.

THE SECOND REPUBLIC
SUMMARY BY JOÃO JOSÉ ALVES DIAS

The military movement of April 25, 1974 was not very ideological in its roots. It was, above all, a protest revolution against the situation in the Armed Forces and the never-ending Colonial War. Gradually, these were joined by political and social concerns. It was a peaceful transition and the revolution elected the carnation as its icon. The hunger for freedom was infectious.

The program introduced by the Armed Forces Movement (MFA) procured: the dismantling of all supreme authorities from the New State; the extinction of the State Police (PIDE-DGS) and political organizations; the arrest of the regime leaders; economic and financial control; amnesty for all political prisoners; the abolition of censorship; the reorganization of the Armed Forces and the military; freedom to create political associations; reinstating ample freedom.

The main political leaders returned from exile. A provisional government was appointed on a temporary basis — an attempt at a national unity, non-fascist government, led by Adelino da Palma Carlos —, as well as a president — general António de Spínola —, while maintaining the National Salvation Junta. There were five provisional governments (from May 1974 to September 1975) where the tendency towards a communist (or communist-sympathizer) Left became more and more pronounced.

António de Spínola resigned in September 1974 and the presidency was given to another military man, general Costa Gomes. In April 1975, the first free elections in 50 years, for the Constitutional Assembly, were held. The sixth and last provisional government was in place from September 1975 to June 1976, and included strong participation from socialists and social-democrats.

By the end of 1975, the Second Republic had achieved: the restoration of public freedoms and fundamental rights (including divorce); the decolonialisation of Guinea-Bissau, Mozambique, São Tomé and Príncipe, Cape Verde and Angola (which entailed the implementation of the same number of independent republics, and the inherent end of the third Portuguese Empire); the break-up of the great monopolies and the nationalization of countless basic companies; an agrarian reform; gradually promoting political consciousness among citizens; the restoration of diplomatic relations with all states. The country's economic situation was, however, dire, and this was evident through: a serious economic and financial setting; rampant and uncontrolled inflation; high unemployment rates; a large number people returning from the ex-colonies; and the disappearance of a university system worthy of that name.

Two years after the revolutionary movement, the country adopted a new constitution (April 1976). General elections (25 April 1976) and the first presidential elections by direct suffrage were held, electing Ramalho Eanes as president (27 June 1976). The Socialist Party was called to form the first Constitutional Government, with Mário Soares as prime-minister. It was this government that, on March 1977, requested that Portugal join the European Economic Community (EEC). The first intervention by the International Monetary Fund (IMF) in Portugal is recorded.

Between 1978 and 1983, there were another seven governments: one in coalition (PS and CDS); three through presidential initiative, and three formed by a pre-electoral alliance (Democratic Alliance). In 1983, the ninth government was formed by the Central Bloc, which resulted from a parliamentary agreement signed by the Socialist and Social-Democratic Parties. The second request for financial assistance from the IMF is recorded. It was during this government that Portugal signed the treaty to join the EEC (June 1985), effective from January 1 1986.

In November 1985, after another general election, Aníbal Cavaco Silva formed his first government. The following February, Mário Soares was elected president. The dissolution of the elected government led to the general elections of July 1987, where the Social-Democratic Party achieved the first overall majority, a result which would be repeated in the general elections of October 1991. The *Cavaquismo* era (from Cavaco Silva) focussed mainly on a policy of economic growth and financial stability, which invested in modernising the country's infrastructures. The economy grew, and inflation went down from 20 per cent to 4 per cent. The period between 1985 and 1995 was also permeated by a tendency towards despotic authoritarianism and to blur the lines between state and the governing party.

In the general elections of October 1 1995, and again in 1999, the Socialist Party came to power. António Guterres led the 13th and 14th Constitutional Governments. This turn towards the Left was confirmed by the election of Jorge Sampaio as president (in 1996 and, again, in 2001). Macau officially became Macau Special Administrative Region (MSAR) of the People's Republic of China (1999). In 2002, Timor had its independence restored as the Democratic Republic of Timor-Leste (this territory, self-proclaimed as independent in 1975, was occupied by Indonesia from 1975 to 2002).

The poor results achieved by the Socialist Party at the council elections of December 2001 led the prime-minister, António Guterres, to resign. After another general election, in March 2002, it was Durão Barroso's turn to form a Social-Democratic government (PSD), through a centre-right coalition with CDS. When he was appointed president of the European Commission, in July 2004, Durão Barroso handed the leadership of PSD to Pedro Santana Lopes, who headed a new coalition government. After four months in government, its disastrous administration, expressed unequivocally by the president of the Republic, led him to dissolve parliament and the 16th Constitutional Government, which led to another general election (February 2005). The Socialist Party achieved its first overall majority at the National Assembly, and José Sócrates was appointed prime-minister of the 17th government.

At the end of Jorge Sampaio's second presidential term, the right-wing candidate, Aníbal Cavaco Silva, was elected president of the Republic, after having led the government for a decade as prime-minister, from 1985 to 1995.

The Socialist Party won the general election of 2009 with a relative majority, and formed the 18th government, but it resigned in March 2011 due to the rejection of its Stability and Growth Programme, dubbed PEC IV. At the June 2011 general election, PSD obtained a relative majority and Pedro Passos Coelho formed the 19th Constitutional Government with «majority parliamentary support» (from CDS), carried out until the end of the mandate. For the third time, Portugal suffered an intervention and was forced to implement an Economic and Financial Adjustment Programme agreed with the European

Commission, the IMF and the European Central Bank. This intervention was heavily felt and had repercussions across the whole of society.

In October 2015, the two governing parties ran as a coalition to the general elections — this coalition took the name of «Portugal à Frente» (*Portugal First*). It won the majority of votes, but it failed to have its programme for the 20th Portuguese Constitutional Government approved in parliament.

Based on three parliamentary agreements — signed bilaterally between the Socialist Party and the left-wing parties with parliamentary representation (the Left Bloc, the Portuguese Communist Party and the Ecological Party «Os Verdes»), and supported by the only elected representative of PAN (People-Animals-Nature) — and also based on the results of the October 2015 elections, the Socialist Party formed the 21st Constitutional Government and appointed António Costa, the party's secretary-general, as prime-minister. He was sworn in on November 26 2015. The political solution found — dubbed *geringonça* (improvised solution) — executed its mandate, and was able to strike a balance between deficit reduction and «social justice issues», although also increasing government debt.

On January 24 2016, Marcelo Rebelo de Sousa was elected president of the Republic, and was sworn in on 9 March of the same year. With his behaviour — the *president of affection* —, he made his influence felt.

Over the course of the Second Republic, Portugal has achieved full international integration and respect, consolidated not only through the various appointments and elections by its citizens for leading positions in international politics, but also through the country's performance in terms of human rights, science, sports, language and culture.

HEADS OF STATE

Monarchy

Afonso Henriques	(prince)		1128-1139
	(king)		1139-1185
Sancho I			1185-1211
Afonso II			1211-1223
Sancho II			1223-1248
	Afonso, regent (*prince regent*)	1245-1248	
Afonso III			1248-1279
Dinis			1279-1325
Afonso IV			1325-1357
Pedro I			1357-1367
Fernando I			1367-1383
Beatriz	(Leonor Teles, *princess regent and governor*)		1383
	João, Master of Aviz, (*prince regent, defender of the kingdom*)		1383-1385
João I			1385-1433
Duarte			1433-1438
Afonso V			1438-1481
	Leonor de Aragão and Pedro, duke of Coimbra, regents (*prince regent*)	1438-1439	
	Pedro, duke of Coimbra, alone (*authority*)	1439-1448	
	João, prince regent	1476-1477	
João II			1481-1495
Manuel I			1495-1521
João III			1521-1557
Sebastião			1557-1578
	Catarina of Áustria, princess regent	1557-1562	
	Cardinal Henrique, prince regent	1562-1568	
Henrique			1578-1580
	5 Governors, headed by Jorge de Almeida, archbishop of Lisbon		1580
António			1580
Filipe I (II of Spain)			1580-1598

cardinal Alberto, viceroy	1583-1593	
5 governors headed by Miguel de Castro, archbishop of Lisbon	1593-1600	
Filipe II (III of Spain)		1598-1621
Cristóvão de Moura, 1st Marquis of Castelo Rodrigo, viceroy	1600-1603	
Afonso de Castelo Branco, bishop of Coimbra, viceroy	1603-1604	
Pedro de Castilho, bishop of Leiria, viceroy	1605-1608	
Cristóvão de Moura, 1st Marquis of Castelo Rodrigo, viceroy	1608-1612	
Pedro de Castilho, bishop of Leiria, viceroy	1612-1614	
Aleixo de Meneses, archbishop of Braga, viceroy	1614-1615	
Miguel de Castro, archbishop of Lisbon, viceroy	1615-1617	
Diogo da Silva e Mendonça 1st Marquis of Alenquer and 1st Duke of Francavila, viceroy	1617-1621	
Filipe III (IV of Spain)		1621-1640
Council of governors, headed by Martinho Afonso Mexia, bishop de Coimbra	1621-1623	
Idem, by Diogo de Castro, 2nd count of Basto	1623-1626	
Idem, by Afonso Furtado de Mendonça, archbishop of Braga and then Lisbon*	1626-1630	
Diogo de Castro, 2nd count of Basto, alone	1630-1631	
António de Ataíde, 1st count of Castro Daire Castanheira and Nuno de Mendonça, 1st count of Vale dos Reis	1631-1632	

* Alone, between 1627 and 1630

	António de Ataíde, 1st count of Castro Daire Castanheira, alone	1632-1633
	José Manuel, archbishop of Lisbon, viceroy	1633
	Council of State, in charge of the governance	1633
	Diogo de Castro, 2nd count of Basto, viceroy	1633-1634
	Margarida de Sabóia, Duchess of Mântua, vice-queen	1634-1640
João IV		1640-1656
Afonso VI		1656-1683
	Luisa of Guzman, princess regent	1656-1662
	Pedro, prince regent	1667-1683
Pedro II		1683-1706
João V		1706-1750
José I		1750-1777
Maria I and Pedro III		1777-1786
Maria I, alone		1786-1816
	João, prince regent (in Brasil since 1808)	1792-1816
	Regency of governors* headed by the 3rd marquis of Abrantes, D. Pedro de Lencastre da Silveira Castelo Branco Sá e Meneses	1807-1808
	French occupation rule	1808
	Regency headed by the bishop of Porto and electer-patriarch of Lisbon, D. António José de Castro	1808-1814
	Idem, by the 1st Marquis of Olhão, Francisco de Melo da Cunha Mendonça e Meneses, or the 2nd Marquis of Borba, Fernando Maria de Sousa Coutinho Castelo Branco e Meneses	1814-1818
	Idem, by the cardinal-patriarch of Lisbon, Carlos da Cunha e Meneses	1818-1820
João VI (in Brazil until 1821)		1816-1826
	António da Silveira Pinto da Fonseca, head of the Provisiosal Meeting of the Supreme Rule of the Kingdom (Porto)	1820

* Variable number

	Gomes Freire de Andrade, Dean of Lisbon Cathedral, head of the interim government (Lisbon)	1820
	Gomes Freire de Andrade, Principal Dean of the Lisbon Cathedral, head of the Provisional Meeting of the Supreme Rule of the Kingdom (Lisbon and Porto)	1820-1821
	Manuel António de Sampaio Melo e Castro Moniz Torres de Lusigan, count of Sampaio, head of the regency	1821
Pedro IV		1826
Maria II		1826-1853
	Isabel Maria, princess regent	1826-1828
	Miguel, prince regent	1828
	Pedro de Sousa Holstein, 1st Marquis of Palmela, head of the regency	1829-1831
	Pedro IV, regent	1831-1834
	Francisco Xavier da Silva Pereira, 1st count of Antas, head of the Provisional Meeting of the Supreme Rule of the Kingdom (Porto)	1846-1847
Miguel I*		1828-1834
Pedro V		1853-1861
	Fernando II**	1853-1855
Luís I		1861-1889
Carlos I		1889-1908
Manuel II		1908-1910

Republic

President of the Interim Government
Joaquim Teófilo Fernandes Braga   1910-1911

---

*   Effective rule over all the continental metropolitan territory from 1828 to 1832; limited rule since the invasion by the supporters of D. Maria II, from 1832 to 1834.
** Nominal king since 1837.

Presidents of the Republic

Manuel de Arriaga Brum da Silveira	1911-1915
Joaquim Teófilo Fernandes Braga	1915
Bernardino Luís Machado Guimarães*	1915-1917

President of the Cabinet

Sidónio Bernardino Cardoso da Silva Pais	1917-1918

Presidents of the Republic

Sidónio Bernardino Cardoso da Silva Pais	1918
João do Canto e Castro Silva Antunes	1918-1919
Henrique Mitchell de Paiva Couceiro, president of the Provisional Meeting of the Kingdom (Porto)	1919
António José de Almeida	1919-1923
Manuel Teixeira Gomes	1923-1925
Bernardino Luís Machado Guimarães	1925-1926

Presidents of the Cabinet

José Mendes Cabeçadas Júnior	1926
Manuel de Oliveira Gomes da Cota	1926
António Óscar de Fragoso Carmona	1926-1928

Presidents of the Republic

António Óscar de Fragoso Carmona	1928-1951
Adalberto Gastão de Sousa Dias, presidente da Junta Governativa (Madeira)	1931

President of the Council (President of the Republic ex officio)

António de Oliveira Salazar	1951

Presidents of the Republic

Francisco Higino Craveiro Lopes	1951-1958
Américo de Deus Rodrigues Tomás	1958-1974
Presidente da Junta de Salvação Nacional António Sebastião Ribeiro de Spínola	1974

* Discharged on December 11, 1917. Resigned functions only on June 2, 1919.

Presidents of the Republic

António Sebastião Ribeiro de Spínola	1974
Francisco da Costa Gomes	1974-1976
António dos Santos Ramalho Eanes	1976-1986
Mário Alberto Lopes Soares	1986-1996
Jorge Fernando Branco de Sampaio	1996-2006
Aníbal António Cavaco Silva	2006-2016
Marcelo Nuno Duarte Rebelo de Sousa	2016-

BIBLIOGRAPHY

ALDEN, Dauril, *Royal Government in Colonial Brazil. With Special Reference to the Administration of the Marquis of Lavradio. Viceroy, 1769-1779*, Berkeley and Los Angeles, University of California Press, 1968.

AXELSON, Eric, *Portuguese in Southeast Africa, 1600-1700*, Johannesburg, Witwatersrand University Press, 1960.

AXELSON, Eric, *Portugal and the Scramble of Africa, 1875-1891*, Johannesburg, Witwatersrand University Press, 1967.

BENTLEY, Duncan T., *Atlantic Islands. Madeira, the Azores and the Cape Verde in Seventeenth-Century Commerce and Navigation*, Chicago-London, The University of Chicago Press, 1972.

BIRMINGHAM, David, *Trade and Conflict in Angola: The Mbundu and Their Neighbours under the Influence of the Portuguese, 1483-1790*, Oxford, Clarendon Press, 1966.

BOXER, Charles Ralph, *The Christian Century in Japan, 1549-1650*, California and Cambridge University Press, 1951.

BOXER, Charles Ralph, *The Dutch in Brazil, 1624-1654*, London, 1956.

BOXER, Charles Ralph, *Fidalgos in Far East, 1550-1770*, 2nd edition, Hague, Hong Kong, Oxford University Press, 1968.

BOXER, Charles Ralph, *The Golden Age of Brazil, 1691-1750*, Berkeley, University of California Press, 1962.

BOXER, Charles Ralph, *The Great Ship from Amacon: Annals of Macao and the old Japan Trade, 1555-1640*, Lisbon, Centro de Estudos Históricos Ultramarinos, 1959.

BOXER, Charles Ralph, *The Portuguese Seaborne Empire, 1415-1825*, London, Hutchinson, 1969-

BOXER, Charles Ralph, *Portuguese Society in the Tropics: The Municipal Councils of Goa, Macao,*

BOXER, Charles Ralph, *Race Relations in the Portuguese Colonial Empire, 1415-1825*, Oxford, Clarendon Press, 1963.

BOXER, Charles Ralph, *Salvador da Sá and the Struggle for Brazil and Angola*, Oxford, 1952.

CHERKE, MARKUS, *Dictator of Portugal: A life of the Marquis of Pombal (1699-1782)*, London, 1938.

CLIILCOTE, Ronald, *Portuguese Africa*, Englewood Cliffs, Prentice Hall, Inc., 1967.

DIFFIE, Bailey, *Prelude to Empire: Portugal Overseas before Henry the Navigator*, University of Nebraska Press, 1960.

Encyclopaedia of Islam, new edition, directed by B. Lewis, Ch. Pellat and T. Schaar Leiden-Paris, Brill, 1960, 6 volumes published.

FRANCIS, A.D., *The Methuens and Portugal, 1691-1708,* Cambridge University Press, 1966.

GODINHO, Vitorino Magalhães, «Portugal and her Empire», in *The New Cambridge Modern History*, vol. V, *The Ascendancy of France, 1648-88,* Cambridge University Press, 1961, pp. 384-397.

GODINHO, Vitorino Magalhães, «Portugal and her Empire, 1680-1720», in *The New Cambridge Modern History*, vol. VI, *The Rise of Great Britain and Russia, 1688-1725,* Cambridge University Press, 1970, pp. 509-540.

HAMMOND, Richard J., *Portugal and Africa, 1815-1910. A Study in Uneconomic Imperialism,* Stanford, Stanford University Press, 1966.

HANSON, Carl. A., *Economy and Society in Baroque Portugal, 1668-1703* The University of Minnesota Press-The Macmillan Press Ltd., 1981.

Kay, Hugh, *Salazar and Modern Portugal,* London, Eyre & Spottiwood, 1970.

KUBLER, G., and SORIA, M., *Art and Architecture in Spain and Portugal and their American Dominions*, Harmondsworth, The Pelican History of Art, 1959.

Letters of John III King of Portugal, 1521-1557, vol. I, ed. by J. D. M. Ford vol. n, ed. by J. D. M. Ford and L. G. Moffatt, Cambridge-Massachusetts, Harvard University Press, 1931-33.

Marques, A H. de Oliveira, *Daily Life in Portugal in the Late Middle Ages*, Madison-Milwaukee-London, The University of Wisconsin Press, 1971.

Marques, A H. de Oliveira, *History of Portugal,* vols. I and II, 2-d edition, New York, Columbia University Press, 1976.

MARTINS, Hermínio, *Portugal,* offprint from *European Fascism,* ed. by S. J. Woolf, London, Weidenfeld and Nicolson, 1968.

OMAN, Charles, *A History of the Peninsular War,* 7 vols., Oxford, 1902-30.

Portuguese Africa. A Handbook, ed. by David M. Abshire and Michael A. Samuels London, Pall Mall Press, 1969.

PRADO, J[or], CAIO, *The Colonial Background of Modern Brazil,* trans. by Suzette Macedo, University of California Press, 1967.

REILLY, Bernard F., *The Kingdom of León-Castilla under Queen Urraca, 1109-1126,* Guilford, Surrey, Princeton University Press, 1982.

REYNOLDS, Robert L., «Reconsideration on the History of the Suevi», in *Revue Belge de Philologie et d'Histoire,* XXXV, n.° 1, 1957.

ROGERS, Francis M., *The Travels of the Infante Dom Pedro of Portugal,* Cambridge Massachusetts, Harvard University Press, 1961.

RUSSELL PETER E., *The English Intervention in Spain and Portugal in the Time of Edward III & Richard II*, Oxford, University Press, 1955.

SAUNDERS A C. de C. M., *A Social History of Black Slaves and Freedmen in Portugal, 1441-1555*, Cambridge University Press, 1982.

SCHWARTZ, STUART B., *Sovereignty and Society in Colonial Brazil. The High Court of Bahia and Its Judges, 1609-1751*, Berkeley, University of California Press, 1973.

SHILLINGTON, Violet M., and CHAPMAN, Annie Beatrice W., *The Commercial Relations of England and Portugal*, London, 1907.

SIDERI, Sandro, *Trade and Power. Informal Colonialism in Anglo Portuguese Relations*, Rotterdam, Rotterdam University Press, 1970.

SMITH, Robert C., *The Art of Portugal, 1500-1800*, New York, Meredith Press, 1968.

STANISLAWSKI, Dan, *The Individuality of Portugal, Study in Historical-Political Geography*, Austin, University of Texas Press, 1959.

WARHUST, Philip R., *Anglo-Portuguese Relations in South-Central Africa, 1890-1900*, London, Longmans, 1962.

WHEELER, Douglas L., *Republican Portugal. A Political History, 1910-1926*, Madison, The University of Wisconsin Press, 1978.

WHEELER, Douglas L., and PÉLISSIER, René, *Angola*, London, Pall Mall Press, 1971.

THE AUTHOR

A.H. de Oliveira Marques (1933-2007) was born in São Pedro do Estoril, Portugal. He received a degree in Historical and Philosophical Sciences from the University of Lisbon and pursued an internship at the University of Wüzburg, in Germany. In 1957, he started teaching at the Faculdade de Letras/University of Lisbon, where he would complete his PhD in 1960. He moved to the USA in 1965 and lectured in Auburn, Florida, Columbia, Minnesota and Chicago until 1970, when he returned to Portugal. He headed the Portuguese National Library (1974-1976) and became a Professor at New University of Lisbon (1976), where he presided the founding commission of the Faculty of Humanities and Social Sciences (1977-1980) and the University's Scientific Council. In 1977, he received an *Honoris Causa* degree from Australian La Trobe University and the president of the Portuguese Republic awarded him with the Grã Cruz da Ordem da Liberdade in 1988. As an historian he authored over 60 books and is considered one of the main experts on Portuguese Medieval History.

A VERY SHORT
HISTORY OF
PORTUGAL

was typeset in Hoefler Text
and Clarendon and printed at Guide,
Artes Gráficas, on 90 g Coral Book
paper in October 2019.

A VERY SHORT
HISTORY
OF PORTUGAL